Aleksander Jankovič Potočnik

ERWIN ROMMEL'S BLUE MAX

or

Just what did Rommel do to deserve the highest German military medal?

Erwin Rommel's Blue Max
or
Just what did Rommel do to deserve
the highest German military medal?

Author: Aleksander Jankovič Potočnik

Editor: Anton Marn
Publisher: Aleksander Jankovič Potočnik

Illustrations: Aleksander Jankovič Potočnik
Photography: Aleksander Jankovič Potočnik
Rafael Marn
National Contemporary History Museum of Slovenia
Bundesarchiv
Haus der Geschichte Baden-Württemberg
Imperial War Museum
Joe E. Kaufmann

Design: Aleksander J. Potočnik, Anton Marn
Proofreading: Elsie B. Hill
Print: CreateSpace, an Amazon.com company

Ljubljana, 2014

Copyright: © Aleksander Jankovič Potočnik, 2014
All rights reserved. No part of this book may be reproduced or transmitted in any form or by any means, electronic or mechanical, including photocopying, recording or by any information storage and retrieval system, without permission from the author in writing - or in case of photographic material without permission from the relevant (listed above) institutions and individuals.

CIP - Kataložni zapis o publikaciji
Narodna in univerzitetna knjižnica, Ljubljana

929Rommel E.
94(497.473)«1917«
355.48(497.473)«1917«

JANKOVIČ Potočnik, Aleksander
    Erwin Rommel's Blue Max or Just what did Rommel do to deserve the highest German military medal? / [author, illustrations] Aleksander Jankovič Potočnik ; [photography Aleksander Jankovič Potočnik ... et al.]. - Ljubljana : author, 2014

ISBN 978-961-283-111-0
275255296

Aleksander Jankovič Potočnik

ERWIN ROMMEL'S BLUE MAX

or

Just what did Rommel do to deserve
the highest German military medal?

CONTENTS

INTRODUCTION

    A PICTURE IN A BOOK 7
    WHY A BOOK? 11

Part 1:
ROMMEL

    YOUTH 15
    THE FIRST WORLD WAR 17
    BETWEEN THE TWO WARS 21
    FRANCE 24
    THE DESERT FOX 26
    UNEMPLOYED 32
    THE ATLANTIC WALL 33
    D-DAY 39
    CONSPIRACY AND DEATH 41

PART 2:
ALONG THE PATH OF THE BREACH

    SOME INTERESTING STATISTICS 43
    THE ROAD TO THE ISONZO FRONT 46
    PREPARATIONS FOR THE OFFENSIVE ... 58
    THE FIRST DAY - OCTOBER 24, 1917 66
    THE SECOND DAY – OCTOBER 25, 1917 .. 75
    THE THIRD DAY – OCTOBER 26, 1917 91
    CHASING THE ENEMY 102

PART 3
HONOUR AND GLORY

   A QUESTION OF HONOUR 111
   INFILTRATION TACTICS 113
   THE QUESTION OF HONOUR -
   THE SECOND TIME 118
   CONCLUSION 123

Sources 124
Archive Material 125
Photographs 125
Ilustrations and Maps 125
About the Author 126
Acknowledgements 127

INTRODUCTION

A PICTURE IN A BOOK

Saturday, November 9th 2013 was a rainy day and I was more than pleased to be able to stay indoors. I was reflecting about some WW1 photo and, since I could no longer recall where I'd seen it, I decided to browse through all the books on my bookshelf related to the period. One of them was titled "Der einsame Krieg" or "The Lonesome War" written by Heinz von Lichem and published in 1999 by Athesia from Bozen (German) or Bolzano (Italian). The subtitle claimed that the book covered the area between the Julian Alps and Joch. On page 169 an illustration caught my eye. Only two years ago I wouldn't have thought much about it. The scene could have really taken place anywhere between Joch and the Julian Alps. But now it rang a bell and after noticing the long barrels of the 149 mm cannons in the picture, I recognised it with certainty. But almost instantly I also noticed discrepancies between what was in the picture and what actually happened in the event.

The foreground of the illustration is dominated by two German soldiers. The nearest one has stopped and is pulling the trigger out of his typical German hand grenade with the stick. The other one, slightly behind the first, is in a dramatic pose throwing his own hand grenade. His rifle is unconvincingly hanging over his knapsack. Clearly theirs are not the first two hand grenades to have been thrown. In the trench on their left, two Italians can be seen. One has already collapsed into the trench while the other is spreading his hands after just being hit by a bullet or by shrapnel. On the right hand side of the picture, a group of German soldiers with rifles in their hands can be seen rushing over the ridge to join the two men in the foreground in their fight against the Italians. In the background there is another advancing group charging over the ridge. Behind this dramatic scene a distant mountain ridge can be discerned. It closely resembles the unmistakable shape of the 2244 metre high Mount Krn.

The illustration is therefore detailed enough to enable us to recognise both the location and the event. But the event didn't happen in exactly the way it is depicted. True, the sky cleared that morning. But no hand grenades were thrown by the attackers and no defender spread out his hands after being shot. Only the 149 mm cannons were probably standing very much as depicted. In reality, the attackers rushed in, all bent forward in the hope of avoiding detection. And so, rather than that of mortal agony it was an expression of utter disbelief and astonishment that gripped the faces of the defenders as the attackers burst into their shelters. But the biggest discrepancy is the caption beneath the illustration. It reads, "The soldiers of the Bavarian Royal Regiment Leib breaking, by the conquest of the Kolowrat Ridge, the last Italian defence line before the Italian lowlands".

This is indeed the ridge of Kolovrat (or Kolowrat in German) where the third Italian line of defence was entrenched. In the rise at the end of the ridge, we can easily recognise the rise of Nagnoj, quote 1192, which means the depicted place really is the spot where the breach of the line opening the gate to the plains of Italy took place. So what's the problem? The problem is that the soldiers of the Leib regiment were at this time actually a kilometre and a half further to the east, trying in vain to conquer the quote 1114 - the rise of Na gradu.

So has a mistake been published in the book? That's something one would be prone to think of first. But no, that's not the case, and when looking further into the matter things really become interesting. Lieutenant Ferdinand Schörer, who commanded the unit of the Leib Regiment attacking the quote 1114 was, for his presumed success in breaking the third defence line, awarded the then highest German military medal *Pour le Merite*. Depicted in the book is therefore the official version of the event according to which the breach was achieved by a unit that was at that very moment one and a half kilometres away from the spot where the breach actually took place. How could recognition be received by someone who had not really been there while the person that should have been given the credit was ignored?

When we set out to write this book we were merely planning to retrace the steps of a historic personality, very much as we did in the book "On Hemingway's trail of the novel A Farewell to Arms" by following the literary routes of the novel's main hero, Frederic Henry. Little did we imagine that answering the above question would become the core of this book. But it couldn't have been any other way, for in reality the soldiers depicted in the illustration, while breaking the last Italian defence line, were not the members of the Leib Regiment, but a company of the 2nd Würtenberg Mountain Hunters Battalion commanded by the then lieutenant, Erwin Rommel.

The difference between the achievements of individual participants in the battle and the way honours were awarded shows how great the dilemma was that the German commanding officers faced after the battle. The roles actually played during the battle were quite different from those assigned to the players in the original battle orders. The unknown author of the illustration probably never realised that he was not only depicting one of the most decisive moments of the 12th Isonzo Battle, but also one of the turning points in the development of military doctrine.

A copy of an illustration by an unknown artist in the book "Der einsame Krieg" or "The Lonesome War" by Heinz von Lichem. Illustration: author.

WHY A BOOK?

A good friend of mine, artist Branko Drekonja, had the odd idea that during the First World War Ernest Hemingway had passed through his village. He arrived at that conclusion after reading his novel "A Farewell to Arms". This, however, was not a self-evident conclusion. In his novel, Hemingway omitted to mention any place names apart from the city of Gorica (Italian: Gorizia). But comparing various descriptions from the novel with the geography of his native valley of the Soča (Isonzo) river, Branko suggested the possible itineraries of the novel's hero, lieutenant Frederic Henry. One of them led from the town of Kanal to the mountain village of Kanalski Vrh, passing Branko's village of Morsko.

A few years ago, the two of us travelled along the three itineraries described in Hemingway's novel and wrote a book about them. Thanks to the support by the Mayor of the township of Kanal, Mr Andrej Maffi, the book was published in 2009 by the Ad Pirum Institute, headed by Mr Anton Marn. The good reception of the Slovenian public prompted us to look for another similar topic. This time we've chosen a real life event - fighting for the ridge of Kolovrat in October 1917 as part of the 12th Isonzo battle. The reason for that were reports that Erwin Rommel, the famous Field Marshal of the Second World War, participated in the fighting as a young lieutenant. Nothing in the reports suggested that Rommel played a particularly significant role in this operation. But just the fact that a person who later became so famous was there seemed good enough reason to look into it and follow the route along which he was fighting.

With the go-ahead by Anton Marn I set out to work, expecting it to be a rather routine affair. First I would gather available sources and collect some archive pictorial material. Then I would trace the route of Rommel's advance along the Kolovrat ridge and document the present appearance of places where the battle had unfolded. In the end all this would be joined in a presentable book. Such was the idea and this was indeed how the work started.

There were many books describing the 12th Isonzo battle in great detail, but none of them mentioned Rommel, except maybe noting that he too was there. As for Rommel's own book about the event, things were described in such minute detail that they hardly made any sense. It wasn't until I started to draw some maps that a clear picture began to emerge. It was becoming clearer and clearer that Rommel's role was far more significant than one could deduct from available sources. Try to make a simple comparison. Imagine a band of medieval soldiers trying to break into a castle. They can't break in, so withstanding the rain of arrows and with boiling oil being poured onto them, they bring a battering ram and little by little break down the door. Once the doors are crushed into splinters, a massacre ensues in the doorway until the attackers finally break in, leaving a pile of dead bodies behind them. But this is not what happened in the case of Kolovrat, where it was as if somebody had sneaked up to the doors and turned the key. The doors then swung open and before the defenders could realise what was going on the attackers had already taken the castle.

The book we were preparing therefore surpassed the original intention of being just a description of Rommel's route and became a story uncovering one of Rommel's biggest military achievements which ultimately brought him the highest German military honour: the medal called *Pur le Merite*.

To tell the story let me first define some of the most important points.

Isonzo Battles (also Battles of the Isonzo)
In 1915 Italy declared war on Austria-Hungary. Its main thrust was directed eastwards, over the Soča river (Isonzo in Italian). Austrian forces dug in along the river and during the next two years they repelled eleven major Italian offensives. The battles exhausted both armies. Fearing a collapse of the Austrian army, the Germans decided to help the Austrians organise and execute a counter-offensive, which started on October 24, 1917. It became known as the 12th Isonzo Battle but also as "The Miracle of Caporetto".

Caporetto
Caporetto is the Italian name for the Slovenian town of Kobarid. Kobarid is one of the three little towns in the upper Soča river valley, the other two being Bovec lying above and Tolmin lying below the Kobarid. It also lies at the top of the bend that the river makes while flowing from Bovec to Tomin. During the 12th Isonzo Battle the Austro-German forces executed a pincer move starting from Bovec and Tolmin and joining at Kobarid, thus cutting off a big portion of the Italian forces. On the third day of the battle, the Italian defence collapsed and they retreated one hundred kilometres westwards to the river Piave. Because of the scale of their victory the Central powers called the battle "The Miracle of Caporetto". On the other hand, ever since then the word "Caporetto" is synonymous in Italian for a complete disaster.

Kolovrat Ridge and Matajur

Kolovrat Ridge is a ridge extending westwards from the city of Tolmin and partly overlooking Kobarid. During the 12th Isonzo battle, it was an area of operation of the German Alpine Corps which included also Erwin Rommel's Württenberg Mountain Hunters Battalion. Further to the west, separated from Kolovrat by the valley of Livek, lies the 1641 metre high peak of Matajur, which overlooks to the west the valley of the river Nadiža – Natissone.

In the period 1915-1917 both the ridge of Kolovrat and the peak of Matajur were used by the Italians as the third and the last line of defence.

Blue Max

Blue Max (*Blauer Max* in German) is a nickname for the highest German military honour, the order *Pour le Merite*. The award was founded in 1740 by the Prussian King Frederick II (known as Frederik the Great) for the recognition of extraordinary personal military achievement. It was awarded solely on the basis of merit, regardless of the social status of the person receiving it. From the very start, it was considered to be the highest possible honour for military achievements and it retained that status also after the unification of Germany. In 1742, a separate form of the order was established for civil achievements. This form still exists while the original military form of the order became extinct with the abdication of the German Emperor, William II, on November 9, 1918. The physical symbol of the award is a golden trimmed blue-enamelled Maltese Cross with golden eagles between the arms. A crown and a letter "F" on the upper arm of the cross stand for the founder of the order, Frederik II. The words: "Pour le Merite" are written over the other three arms.

Part 1
ROMMEL

YOUTH

Erwin Rommel was born on November 15, 1891 in Heidenheim on the river Brenz. He was the second son of a high school teacher Erwin Rommel and his wife Helena, born in Luz. Both of his parents were of Lutheran faith. In his application to the military school young Erwin Rommel wrote that he had fond memories of his childhood. What he omitted to say was that his first choice of career was engineering rather than the military. He and one of his friends even assembled a glider. Later he would tell those close to him: "It actually flew - though not very far." [1]

Later, he would also say that he and his father were never really close. Yet it was his father who decided that his son's best future was in the army. Without hesitation he covered the expenses of the hernia surgery that the army officials deemed necessary if the boy was to enrol in a military school. Here it is worth noticing that the Rommels were not a military family. Erwin's older brother Karl enrolled in the army only to avoid the matriculation exam and later became a well reputed pilot, while his younger brother Gerhardt became an opera singer. So it would appear that his father simply discerned his son's abilities well.

Due to his ill health, young Erwin was at first rejected

---

[1] David Irwing: The Trail of the Fox, Hoffman und Campe Verlag, Hamburg 1978

Above: Cadet Erwin Rommel photographed while reading a book (1910). Courtesy of: Haus der Geschichte Baden-Württemberg.

Below: Erwin Rommel with Lucie Mollin whom he met as a cadet at a dance in the Officer's Club in Danzig (1911). Courtesy of Haus der Geschichte Baden-Württemberg.

by the artillery and the pioneers. After his father organised surgery, the youngster was finally accepted into the Infantry Regiment No 124 (2). He joined it on June 19, 1910. In 1911, he had training in Danzig and on completing it, he became a lieutenant. During the training, cadets were allowed to attend dances in the officer's club. During one such "official dance" he met a female student, Lucie Mollin. She became the love of his life. They were married five years later, in 1916, while Rommel was on leave in Danzig. When he became famous, he liked to tease her with letters sent to him by his female admirers. But it would appear that he remained faithful to her until his premature death in 1944.

For two years, Rommel trained recruits in his 124th Regiment, stationed in Weingarten in Upper Swabia, but on March 1st, 1914 he was transferred to the 49th Field Artillery Regiment in Ulm. With international tensions growing, Rommel asked to be transferred back to the men he was training with. He arrived back at the 124th Regiment just shortly before the outbreak of hostilities.

THE FIRST WORLD WAR

Rommel spent the first two years of the Great War on the Western Front. He immediately excelled with courage and initiative. Once he found himself facing three French soldiers without any ammunition left. He charged with the bayonet. "I knew I shouldn't had given them time to react or else I'd be shot," he later explained calmly. In September 1914, he was wounded near Varennes and sent to hospital. For his brave service he received the Iron Cross 2nd Class. In January 1915,

---

(2) Infantry Regiment No 124 was also named Württemberg Infantry Regiment No 6 and the Infantry Regiment of King William I.

he was back at the 124th Regiment, which was then stationed in Aragonne.

In October 1915, Rommel was transferred to a newly established Württenberg Mountain Battalion (3) under the command of Major Theodor Sprösser. They trained in the Arlberg region of Austria. In the beginning of 1916, they were sent to the High Vosges, where a daring breach into the enemy line earned Rommel the Iron Cross 1st Class. In October, the WGB was sent to Romania. They endured encounters in harsh winter conditions which often claimed more victims than the enemy. On August 9, the battle for Mount Cosna began. While the battle lasted even longer, the WGB was engaged until August 25. At the very onset of the battle Rommel for the first time executed a flanking manoeuvre which opened the door for the troops that had previously attacked frontally unsuccessfully. Soon afterwards Rommel was lightly wounded, but held on until August 20. It was probably during these eleven days of battle for Mt Cosna that Rommel and Major Sprösser forged their mode of operation and a mutual trust that brought about their amazing success at Kolovrat Ridge.

Rommel's WGB arrived at the Soča (Isonzo) battlefield in October 1917 as a part of the German 14th Army under the command of General Otto von Bellow. The task of Bellow's army was to help the Austrians breach the Italian front and remove the danger of an Austrian collapse. After eleven Italian offensives, the Austrians were brought to the brink of exhaustion and their ability to sustain another such onslaught was highly questionable. Together with the Bavarian Infantry Regiment Leib and 1st Hunters Battalion, WGB formed the Alpine Corps. The Corps was to advance along the line Tolmin, Kolovrat, Matajur (Monte Maggiore), Cividale. Rommel's WGB was to protect the right flank of the Bavarian Leib Regiment.

---

(3) WGB stands for the original German version of the name of the unit: Württembergisches Gebirgs Regiment.

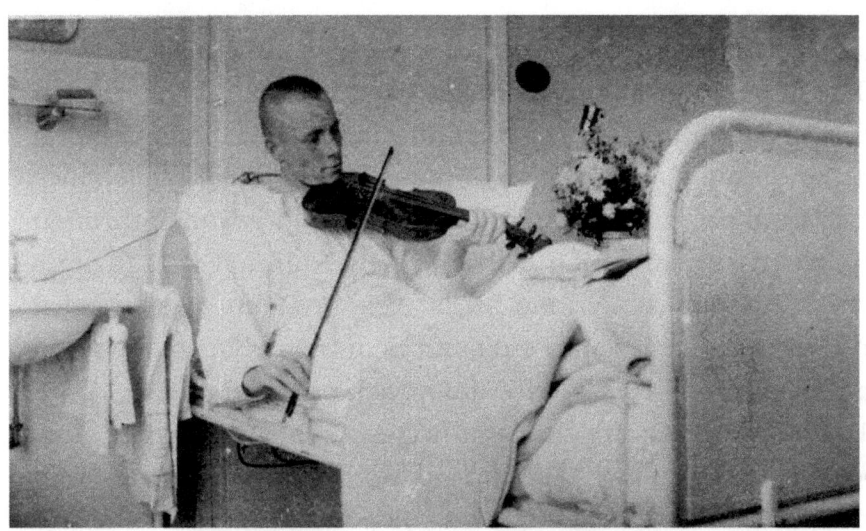

Above: Erwin Rommel recuperating in Stuttgart after being wounded for the first time in September 1914. Courtesy of: Haus der Geschichte Baden-Württemberg.

Below: Theodor Sprösser, the superior, and his trusted subordinate, Erwin Rommel. Besides the effective use of infiltration tactics, it was their mutual trust and consequent effective co-operation that resulted in splendid victories on Kolovrat and Matajur. Courtesy of Haus der Geschichte Baden-Württemberg.

During the operation that became known in history as "The Miracle of Caporetto" the breach of the Italian front unfolded with incredible speed. It may be that the motivation of the young German officers played a significant role since they were promised high honours for rapid advance through the enemy lines, which explains why Rommel was furious when the highest German medal *Pour le Merite* was awarded to Bavarian Lieutenant Ferdinand Schörner who, as envisaged in the original plan, led a frontal attack on the quote 1114 (Na Gradu). He was sure that the Italian crew surrendered only because he managed to cut it from the rear. Rommel was even more upset when he conquered the peak of Matajur. General Bellow personally promised *Pour le Merite* to the first officer to reach the peak. But rather than to Rommel, the medal went to the Silesian Lieutenant Walter Schnieber, who was nowhere in sight at the time of Rommel's conquest. As it turned out Schnieber seized only a nearby quote 1325. But Rommel's official complaint received no answer.

In three decisive days, Rommel's detachment took 9000 prisoners, 150 of whom were officers, and 84 cannons, while their own losses were five fallen soldiers, one fallen officer and 30 wounded. True, the low morale of the Italian soldiers played an important role in this success of Rommel's. As he wrote later on, things changed considerably at Monte Grappa. The Italians knew they were defending their own soil there and fought courageously. But it was only in Africa during the Second World War that he really changed his opinion about Italian soldiers. He found out first hand then that the incompetence of their leadership was the main cause of their inefficiency.

Once the front line was breached, the attackers pursued the retreating Italians all the way to the river Piave. At Longarone, Rommel's unit, advancing well ahead of the army's main body, crossed the river Piave and established a bridgehead. By doing so he blocked a retreat route for all the

Italian troops coming down the valley. Even though they were far superior in numbers, these troops did not manage to break through.

A few days later, German reinforcements arrived and more than 8000 Italian soldiers surrendered. Rommel's own losses were 13 fallen soldiers and one officer who was killed by accident while climbing the mountain slope.

Finally, Rommel's exploits were recognised. The German Emperor awarded him *Pour le Merite* for his conduct at Kolovrat, Matajur and Longarone. Rommel believed that this was a remedy for an injustice he suffered after the conquest of the peak of Mount Matajur. But during the Second World War, he liked to tease his Italian allies with the event at Longarone. So it is no surprise that the city of Longarone now promotes itself as the sole location where Rommel earned his prestigious *Blue Max*.

BETWEEN THE TWO WARS

At the end of the First World War, Erwin Rommel was a captain in the head-quarters of the army corps. During the unrest that followed the war, he was transferred to the 32nd Security Company in Friedrichshafen. The fact that during this troublesome period he managed to avoid bloodshed may well have contributed to his later "unattained" popularity. When sent to put down a rebellion in the town of Schwaebish Gmünd, for example, he decided to use fire engines rather than cannons. After the signing of the Versailles treaty, most German officers were demobilised, but Rommel was allowed to remain in the army and in 1920 he took over command of the company of the Infantry Regiment in Stuttgart.

In 1927, he and his wife Lucie made a motorcycle trip to Northern Italy. Rommel's desire to visit the sites where he fought

Erwin Rommel with a young fox (1914). Could he have imagined then that three decades later he too would be called a fox? Courtesy of Haus der Geschichte Baden-Württemberg.

was hindered by a hostile reception. Word has it that the couple was actually chased out of Longarone.

In 1929, Rommel was posted to an infantry school in Dresden. He was noted for teaching his cadets to avoid unnecessary casualties. "The more a soldier sweats, the less he bleeds!" was his motto. But very much as receiving *Pour le Merite* had done during the war, now his popularity among the students evoked envy among his lecturer colleagues.

In 1933, he became a commander of the Hunting Battalion of the 17th Infantry Regiment in Goslar. It was here that, in 1934, acting as the commander of the guard of honour, he first met Hitler. But Hitler noticed Rommel two years later, during the National Socialist Party gathering in Nuremberg where Rommel was responsible for Hitler's security. In 1937 Rommel published his book "Infantry Attacks" (German original: "Infanterie grieft an"), which brought him both great

A house in Wiener Neustadt, photographed in 1938, which was the home of the Rommel family while Rommel was a commander of a military school there. Courtesy of Haus der Geschichte Baden-Württemberg.

popularity and significant royalties. Popular with the youth, Rommel was considered an ideal representative of the German High Command (OWK) to the National Socialist Youth organisation called Hitlerjugend. But Rommel and Hitlerjugend leader Baldur von Schirach soon disliked each other and in 1938, von Schirach demanded that Rommel be called off.

To compensate for this rebuke, Rommel was named Head of the Security Detachment on Hitler's travels. The two soon established a very good rapport. After the annexation of Austria, Rommel was named Commander of the prestigious Austrian military school in Wiener Neustadt, but Hitler kept calling him to head the security unit on his travels. Apparently it was Rommel who engineered Hitler's journey to Prague, which sealed the German takeover of Czechoslovakia in 1939.

During the attack on Poland, Rommel, who by then already held the rank of Major General, was again heading Hitler's personal guard. Witnessing the efficiency of German tank units, he asked Hitler for the command of an armoured division. This represented a sort of rank-jumping, but Hitler granted his wish.

FRANCE

After the German invasion of Poland on September 1, 1939 England and France formally fulfilled their obligations and declared war on Germany, but did little else. Their inactivity gave Hitler time to thoroughly prepare his next move. During these preparations the mutual respect between Hitler and Rommel deepened. As opposed to the German General Staff, Rommel believed that Hitler's plan for a strong surprise attack had merit and would succeed. This disagreement with the opinion of the General Staff may well explain the good relation between Rommel and Hitler. Both of them were "outsiders": neither Hitler as a politician and a self-made warlord, nor Rommel as a "hands-on commander" reached his position and rank through the general-staff school or through activity in the General Staff, but either by fighting on the battlefield or through politics. They both despised the members of the General Staff to the same extent as the members of the General Staff either despised or envied the two of them.

The German attack on France commenced on May 10, 1940. The unfolding of events was stunning; more so since the French and their British allies had considerable numerical superiority. 156 allied divisions with 4000 tanks were there to meet the attack of 136 German divisions with 2800 tanks. But throughout the campaign, the initiative remained on the German side. By invading Belgium and the Netherlands, the Germans first lured the majority of the allied forces to the north and then cut it off with a sudden and rapid thrust of armoured units from Ardennes towards the English Channel.

The rapid advance of armoured columns nick-named a "blitzkrieg" had many possible shortcomings. The supply lines were becoming extremely extended and in the event of serious engagement, the advancing troops could easily run out of ammunition, fuel and provisions. An experienced and composed opponent could easily attack the exposed flank of the advancing columns, cut them into segments and destroy them one by one. But commanders like Heinz Guderian, Erich von Manstein, Gerd von Rundstedt, Paul Ludwig Ewald von Kleist and also Erwin Rommel consciously opted to take the risk. Just as in Romania and the Soča valley, Rommel would exploit any opening he could identify and advance, regardless of the security of his flanks and contact with the bulk of his army.

During the May war in France, his 7th Division, that was a part of General Hoth's 15th Armoured Corps, advanced an average of 80 to 90 kilometres per day. Because of its speed, night advances and a tendency of appearing on locations where it was least expected, it soon acquired a nickname "the Ghost Division".

With thrust from the flanks, an experienced opponent could easily endanger, cut off and destroy advancing columns. But nothing of the kind happened. Instead a panic spread among the allied troops, followed by a collapse once the German points had reached the Channel coast. In an amazing self-sacrificial effort, British seamen managed to evacuate 215.000 British and 123.000 French soldiers from the coastal town of Dunkerque while France capitulated on June 25, only six weeks after the beginning of the attack. Erwin Rommel was one of the great winners. But just as at the Isonzo Front, he was only one of many. The time of the glory that was to be his and his alone was yet to come.

THE DESERT FOX

The real opportunity to show his worth came for Rommel with German involvement in Northern Africa. In September 1940, the Italians attacked Egypt from Libya and reached the city of Sidi Barrani. Rather than advancing further they dug in. This gave the British commander Archibald Wavell a chance to regroup and counter-attack. By December 1940 he reached the city of El Aghella in Libya and took 100,000 Italian prisoners of war. Simultaneously the British attacked Abyssinia and took it after twelve months of surprisingly vicious fighting

Meanwhile Mussolini attacked Greece from Albania. Despite double Italian superiority, the Greeks repelled the attack and even endangered Italian positions in Albania. In order to help the Greeks eliminate the Italians, the British sent their forces from Libya to Greece. An Italian defeat seemed inevitable, so Hitler decided to help his ally. Meanwhile a military coup in Yugoslavia caused that country to abandon the alliance with the Germans. So, in April, Hitler attacked both Yugoslavia and Greece at the same time. The invasion was swift and successful, but it nevertheless had some fatal consequences. Because of the attack on Greece and Yugoslavia, Hitler had to delay a German attack on the Soviet Union for a whole month, which turned out to be long enough for his plans to fail.

The Germans didn't know that at the time. But they did know that by conquering Yugoslavia and Greece they gained access to the Mediterranean which enabled them to undertake the expulsion of the British from the area. With a pincer movement, with one prong advancing through Egypt and another over the Caucasus, they could then seize the valuable oil fields of the Near East.

Envisaging such a development, Hitler had, as early as February 1941, sent Rommel to the Libyan port of Tripolis to do all the necessary groundwork for such an operation. After the fall of Greece, the British forces retreated to Crete. The Germans caught up with them and after two weeks of fighting captured Crete and 18,000 British defenders. Only 15,000 British soldiers were successfully evacuated. With the fall of Crete, the Germans felt they could start their North African campaign.

Rommel started his advance from Libya in March 1941. His Africa Corps then numbered 16,000 men and about 100 tanks, supported by numerous Italian forces. The British lines at El Aghella were easily breached and Rommel's Corps reached the Egyptian border in no time. In the process, he bypassed and left surrounded the port city of Tobruk, defended by an Australian garrison. Twice British Commander General Archibald Wavell ordered a relief of Tobruk and twice Rommel repulsed the British forces. The British were especially puzzled by Rommel's ability to take advantage of the open terrain, outflank them and attack from behind. The British press started to call him "The Desert Fox". British officers were upset by Rommel's growing fame, but found it also an acceptable excuse for their own lack of success - it's hard to beat a better man.

When it came to the Near East, the views of the British Prime Minister Winston Churchill and those of General Archibald Wavell often collided. So futile attempts to relieve Tobruk gave Churchill an excuse to dismiss Wavell and appoint General Claude Auchinleck. The new commander started the "Operation Crusader" and after a month of heavy fighting forced Rommel to retreat. Tobruk was saved and Rommel pushed back to his starting point at El Raghella. Even though Auchinleck ordered the construction of the new defensive line of Gazala near Tobruk he was sure that Rommel was beaten. His counterattack on January 1942 was therefore a complete surprise. During his advance towards Gazala, Rommel met almost no resistance. Only at Gazala a harsh battle erupted. Auchinleck tried to envisage and counter Rommel's flanking

Above: German »Panzer II« of the Africa Corps. Source: Bundesarchiv, Bild 101I-783-0110-12/Dörner CC-BY-SA.

Below: Erwin Rommel at the meeting with members of his staff during the North African campaign. Source: Bundesarchiv/CC-BY-SA.

manoeuvres. But Rommel's troops prevailed and the British were forced to retreat. Hitler awarded Rommel for the victory by promoting him to Field Marshal.

Auchinleck stopped at El Alamein. This was a spot on the Egyptian border where the passable terrain was narrowed between the sea and the impassable Qattara Depression. Auchinleck hoped that in the narrow straits Rommel would not be able to execute his characteristic flanking manoeuvres. His assumption proved to be correct. Rommel reached British lines on July 1, 1942. Auchinleck managed to sustain all Rommel's assaults and soon the shortage of ammunition and fuel forced Rommel to retreat and dig in. Now Auchinleck counter-attacked, but Rommel's lines held. After a month of exhausting fighting, the situation remained unchanged.

Losing patience over the stalemate Churchill recalled Auchinleck and named two men in his place. General Harold Alexander became the commander for the Near East and General Bernard Montgomery the commander of the 8th Army.

But the armies were entrenching themselves and it was becoming clear that the ability to bring in sufficient reinforcements was to be a decisive issue. Just as the fall of Crete represented a go-ahead sign for the Germans, retaining the island of Malta now became a key issue for the Allies since from Malta they were able to interrupt German supply lines. The Axis powers were aware of the danger. The Italians bombed Malta as early as summer 1940. In 1941, Malta became the target of German bombers. Soon the Germans were also intensely attacking convoys bringing supplies to the island. But despite heavy losses, Malta did not fall and in autumn 1942, the allies started to use Malta as a base for the interception of German supplies.

Meanwhile Rommel acquired a new enemy of which he was not even aware. The British military intelligence managed to obtain the German encrypting machine Enigma and decipher German messages. Not only had Montgomery gathered vastly superior force, but he now knew in advance every move of Rommel's. So when on August 30, 1941 Rommel started his new offensive, Montgomery was ready. He knew Rommel would try to use the Alam El Halfa ridge for his flanking manoeuvre and had it extensively fortified. Rommel crashed into defences he wasn't expecting and after three days his onslaught wore off. Apart from the advance knowledge of Rommel's plans, the British superiority in the air also played a vital role in Rommel's defeat.

Rommel dug in again and asked for reinforcements, but his pleas to Berlin were in vain. The reason was not only the endangered supply routes, but also the fact that for Hitler Africa was increasingly becoming a battlefield of secondary importance. Meanwhile Montgomery kept piling up his reinforcements.

It was October 23, 1942, one day short of the 25th anniversary of Rommel's victorious engagement in the "Miracle of Caporetto", that Montgomery attacked, starting the Second Battle of El Alamein. Short of fresh troops and supplies Rommel knew that he had no other option but to face the inevitable. After ten days of fighting his lines were breached and his Africa Corps was forced to withdraw. At a luncheon in London's Mansion House, Winston Churchill celebrated this first major allied victory by saying, "Now this is not the end. This is not even the beginning of the end. But it is, perhaps, the end of the beginning."

For two months, Montgomery followed Rommel's retreating force closely. Meanwhile Anglo-American forces undertook Operation "Torch" – landings in Morocco and Algeria. Now Rommel also had to consider an attack from behind. Finally some reinforcements arrived and in February 1943 Rommel fortified himself in Tunisia, on the former French defensive line called Mareth. But his plans for a counter-offensive were again deciphered by British Intelligence and relayed to his opponent Montgomery. During the battle of Medenina on March 6, 1943, rather than achieving a surprise, the German tanks rolled into a trap. Rommel realised that the situation became hopeless. On March 9, he handed over the command to general Hans-

This highly symbolic photo shows British Crusader tank advancing past the burning German tank. Source: Imperial War Museum, London.

Jürgen von Arnim and flew to Berlin to convince Hitler to pull his forces out of Africa. But as in every similar situation, Hitler refused the idea of retreat, demanding German soldiers to fight until the last man. Meanwhile the Allies were closing in. On May 7, American forces took the port of Bizerte. On the same day, the British 7th Armoured Division entered the city of Tunis. Five days later, on May 13, 250,000 encircled German and Italian soldiers surrendered. Three days earlier, in a confidential conversation, Hitler supposedly admitted to Rommel, "I should have listened to you. But I suppose it's too late now."

Surprisingly enough this painful military defeat didn't diminish Rommel's reputation. German propaganda continued to glorify him while in the West he was respected for both his military skills and his apparent high moral standards. As opposed to other German commanders, Rommel would not tolerate the maltreatment of the civilian population in occupied areas, he did not approve of forced labour and did not allow the persecution of different ethnic groups. Even in cases of sabotage and active resistance he restrained his troops from massive retaliatory measures that were otherwise a rule rather than an exception.

UNEMPLOYED

Nobody in Berlin was quite sure what to do with the Desert Fox, especially since his reputation was not quite consistent with the outcome of the African campaign. For almost four months he was left without any notable assignment. True, Hitler accepted him in his headquarters where they had some long discussions. Rommel may have well been the only person who, during these conversations, dared to mention the possibility that Germany could lose the war. Hitler's statement that "If they aren't capable of winning the war, the German people deserve to perish." upset Rommel to the extent that he once said to his son Manfred: "'Sometimes you get a feeling that the man is no longer completely normal." But despite keeping company with the "Führer", Rommel, who was used to the battlefield, felt pushed aside.

On July 10, 1943 the Allies landed on Sicily. Hitler considered sending Rommel to command the German forces in Italy. But meanwhile the British successfully carried out an intelligence operation "Mincemeat". They convinced the Germans that the next landing would take place in either Greece or Sardinia. Hitler decided to name Rommel a commander of Army Group E in Greece and sent him off to organise a defence against the invasion. Rommel spent only two days in Greece. After the landing on Sicily, Mussolini's position became unstable and soon afterwards he was removed from power. Hitler planned to occupy Italy in case the new government decided to change sides and Rommel seemed an ideal choice for such an operation. Rommel was summoned back to Berlin and appointed a Commander of the newly formed Army Group B whose task was to defend Northern Italy. But since the new Italian government was still hesitating, Hitler decided not to provoke the Italians who still remembered Rommel's role in their defeat in the First World

War. Meanwhile the commander of Army Group C, field-marshal Kesselring started to doubt Rommel's plan to defend only the northern part of Italy. He argued that from airports established in central Italy, allied bombers could easily reach southern Germany. He claimed that he could defend Rome until 1944.

On September 8 the Allies landed at Salerno and the Italian government capitulated. By then, Kesselring had already managed to convince Hitler to hand over the command of German forces in Italy to him. So instead of Italy Rommel was sent to Normandy.

THE ATLANTIC WALL

Once France was conquered, it seemed clear that the next German target would be Great Britain. During the summer and autumn of 1940, German air forces viciously attacked British military targets, and later also English towns, with the aim of paving the path for the land invasion. Even today, it is unclear just how serious Hitler's plans for the invasion of England really were. But the invasion was surely no longer an option once the German air offensive failed to bring the expected results.

At any rate, cut from the rest of Europe, Britain didn't really present a serious threat and in 1941 Hitler turned the other way and attacked the Soviet Union. Britain seemed isolated and harmless. Things changed on December 7, 1941 when Japan carried out the attack on Pearl Harbour, thus bringing the United States into the war. Without any apparent reason, probably just out of solidarity with his Japanese allies, Hitler declared war on the US. Now it was only a question of time as to when the Allies would use Britain as a base for an invasion of the European continent. Since the occupation of

The construction of the Atlantic Wall fortifications was Germany's great propaganda feat. On the photo, battery Lindemann. Courtesy of Joe E. Kaufmann.

Britain was no longer possible the only remaining measure against the invasion was to fortify the entire Atlantic coast. This was an immense task since the Germans had to secure an excessively long line running along the coast of Norway, Denmark, the Netherlands, Belgium and France before reaching the Spanish border. Once the Germans were defeated in Africa, the French Mediterranean coast had to be defended as well.

The construction of fortifications was entrusted to the private construction firm Todt. Before the war, this company specialised in large infrastructure projects. Until 1938, their main field of work were freeways, the famous "Autobahns". But after that year, their expertise was increasingly used for military objects, among which the fortifications of the Atlantic Wall and V1 and V2 launching sites became their most well-known endeavours. The name Organisation Todt may be misleading. Apart from using the labour force supplied by them, the Organisation had little to do with the skull symbol of the SS units. It was named after the company's founder and owner Fritz Todt, a civil engineer and important member of the German National Socialist Party. But to carry out the seemingly impossible task of fortifying the Atlantic coast, an almost unlimited source of cheap labour, composed mainly of prisoners of war and forced labourers from occupied countries, was made available to the Organisation.

Soon, mighty concrete bunkers were erected on the most strategic points, housing heavy calibre naval guns. In the year 1943, German propaganda claimed the Atlantic Wall to be a formidable defensive belt consisting of 12,000 heavy bunkers and 15,000 fortified defensive posts manned by 300,000 active soldiers and 150,000 reservists. These impressive numbers were to deter an allied invasion. But they even failed to convince Hitler himself. He charged Rommel with the task of determining the actual defensive value of the Atlantic wall and, if necessary, to suggest some improvements.

So besides the rank of Field-Marshal, Rommel was now also given the title of "General Inspector of Atlantic Defensive Structures". It may sound strange that the man, who was so good at conquering fortified positions, was now put in charge of constructing them. But both constructing the fortifications and conquering them demand the same virtue: a profound understanding of fortifications. The case of the famous French fortification architect Sébastien Le Prestre de Vauban is well known. He was an architect first, but later the king asked him to lead some sieges. It was similar with Rommel, but in a different order: a conqueror of fortifications to begin with, he was now asked to construct them.

Rommel started his new task with a thorough inspection trip which was well publicised by the German propaganda machine. He travelled along the entire defensive line: from the Norwegian north to the Pyrenees. He summed up his conclusion in a word: 'unsatisfactory'. Individual bunkers may have indeed been mighty, but they were spread too far apart to represent a continuous defensive line. The fighting value of the troops was also low. Many of them were mobilised in conquered countries and clearly lacked motivation to defend Germany. The other issue was armament. The number of weapons may have been great, but they were scrambled together from all over Europe and many of them were outdated. The ammunition was diverse and in many cases in very short supply.

Rommel knew that he had neither time nor enough resources available to fulfil the giant task in a manner originally envisaged. He therefore chose to massively utilise the simplest possible means: on land, endless quantities of barbed wire; on the beaches and in the coastal belt with changing tides, he ordered a creation of entire forests of simple obstacles against both boats and armoured vehicles. They came in all sorts of shapes. Obstacles welded together from steel beams were transported from Czechoslovakia and concrete pyramid-shaped obstacles forming the "dragon's teeth". As the name implies, notable quantities of "Belgian Doors", interlocked movable anti-tank obstacles, were brought from fortifications in Belgium. But the simplest and at the same time most numerous obstacles were wooden poles driven into the ground at an angle and equipped with either a cutting blade or a mine at the top. In fact, Rommel considered mines to be one of the simplest and yet one of the most efficient means of defence – either when incorporated in mine fields or as a part of an obstacle. It is believed that it was under his command that the first non-metal and therefore undetectable mines were used. In Rommel's case they were made of massive glass.

In the spring of 1944, the progress was evident enough for Rommel to breathe a sigh of relief, even though many locations were still inadequately protected. He concentrated his efforts on the areas where the allied invasion seemed most likely to occur. The first such area was around Calais. Here the British Channel is at its narrowest and crossing it wouldn't take much time. The way to the German industrial heartland also seemed the shortest from the Calais area. Another possible area, at least in Rommel's view, was Normandy. But everybody on the German side, including Rommel himself, believed Calais to be the most likely choice, mainly because there were port facilities available which were essential to bring in all the supplies necessary for the thrust into Germany.

But neither Rommel nor his officers knew that allied planning went the other way. They based their plans on the experience of the Dieppe landing of August 19, 1942. That landing was a politically motivated action aimed at demonstrating to the Soviets their will to open the second front. The goal was limited: the Allies should take the port and hold it long enough for all the port facilities to be destroyed. Then the landing force should retreat. The operation was a great disaster. The attack broke up on the coast and more than half of the attackers were wounded, killed or captured. But while the German propaganda glorified the victory and paraded the multitude of captured allied soldiers in front of the cameras, the Allies drew some valuable conclusions. One of the most important ones was the recognition that armoured vehicles cannot really operate on pebbles, which were characteristic of the area around Calais. In this regard, the fine sand of Normandy beaches was much more favourable. But, as Rommel correctly concluded, there were no appropriate ports in Normandy. What he did not know was that the Allies had developed floating docks made of concrete that could be assembled on the spot into the so-called "Mulberry Ports". The capacity of such a port was 10,000 tons per day. The Allies also improved landing crafts, especially those capable of carrying armoured vehicles. Now all that remained was to convince the Germans that the landing would happen exactly where it was expected – in the Calais area. To achieve that impression the Allies undertook an extensive intelligence operation code-named "Fortitude". False intelligence reports

Above: Raising obstacles on the Belgian coast. Source: Bundesarchiv, Bild 101I-297-1716-28/Schwoon/CC-BY-SA.

Below: Obstacles on the Pas de Calais beach. Source: Bundesarchiv, Bild 101I-719-0240-05/Jesse/CC-BY-SA.

and large quantities of war materials and forces were to suggest a concentration of the army on the coast opposite Calais. In reality, there were only small units, rotating from post to post and producing a lot of fake radio traffic. Masses of dummy vehicles made of wood or even rubber were also used.

Operation "Fortitude" did have a desired effect. But inner German squabbles also worked in the Allies' favour. During fighting in Africa, Rommel recognised the importance of superiority in the air. Knowing that the Allies would have it, he demanded the armoured units to be as close to the coast as possible. Once the invasion starts, he argued, the Allied planes will not allow German tanks to reach the battlefield. The General Staff was of a different opinion. The final decision was made by Hitler who put the armoured units under his personal command. That proved fatal, since on the morning of the invasion no member of his staff dared to wake him up. By the time, he finally gave the order for the tanks to move, it was already too late.

D-DAY

In the summer of 1944 the weather forecast for July was bad. Since he didn't expect the invasion to take place in bad weather, Rommel decided to travel to Berlin. He hoped to persuade Hitler to reinforce the armoured units and move them closer to the coast. At the same time, he planned to call in to see his wife who had a birthday on July 6. But unlike their German counterparts, the British meteorologists predicted a short improvement on that very same July 6. The Supreme Commander of the Allied Forces, general Dwight Eisenhower, gave an order to start the invasion.

The allies had successfully convinced the Germans that the target of the invasion would be Calais. So even after the first reports of the Allied landing had arrived, the Germans were still waiting for a "real" landing to begin. Rommel was absent. Hitler's staff did not dare to wake Hitler up and nobody else was allowed to give the order to move the armoured units forward. Fateful hours passed and the Allies managed to reach the shore and solidify their grip on the beachheads. They successfully created a base for further advance.

Once it was clear that the Allies could no longer be pushed off the coast of Normandy both Rommel and the commander of the Army Group A, Field Marshal Gerd von Rundstedt arrived at the same conclusion that Germany could no longer win the war. On two consecutive meetings with Hitler, one in France and the other in Hitler's Alpine retreat in Bertesgaden, they tried to convince Hitler to allow a retreat of the German troops from Normandy. They also asked him to consider some political solutions that could bring about the end of hostilities. Rommel especially was very direct. Hitler fiercely declined any notion of suing for peace. Von Rundstedt was removed from the post and replaced by Field Marshal Günther von Kluge while, oddly enough, Rommel suffered no consequences.

Upon his arrival in France, Kluge clashed with Rommel. The argument displayed Rommel's usual self-confidence. Reportedly the dialogue went like this:

> von Kluge: "From now on you will have to learn to obey orders like everybody else!"
> Rommel: "How dare you? You are talking to a colleague Field-marshal."
> von Kluge: "You've never commanded a unit bigger than a division."
> Rommel: "And you've never fought the English."

But once von Kluge familiarised himself with the conditions in Normandy he had no other choice but to admit that Rommel's appreciation of the situation was a valid one. He agreed for Rommel to draft a special report for

Army Headquarters and Hitler. The report amounted to an ultimatum. Von Kluge was to send it to the Headquarters, but he hesitated. By the time he gathered enough courage to send the report, events had already overtaken the two Field Marshals.

CONSPIRACY AND DEATH

As early as February 2, 1942, when the entire German 6th Army surrendered at Stalingrad, many Germans realised that Hitler was leading Germany to a disaster. Among them were many army officers. Small groups of conspirators emerged and cautiously spread their networks until, in the summer of 1944, they organised a plot with the aim of overthrowing Hitler and achieving a separate peace with the Western Allies. One of the conspirators was also Rommel's chief of staff, General Hans Speidel. Thanks to him the conspirators were familiar with Rommel's views. They also knew that Rommel was one of the very few German commanders that the Allies would be willing to talk to. Because of that they tried to win him to their side. Even though imminent military defeat and reports of mass crimes had shaken Rommel's trust in Hitler, he did not join the plot. But he did not oppose it either. He only opposed the notion of killing Hitler. For Rommel a trial seemed more appropriate. Their first contacts with Rommel encouraged the conspirators and their plans with Rommel were far bigger than Rommel himself was aware of.

On July 17, a group of British planes attacked Rommel's car on an open road in France. Rommel was heavily wounded and had no influence on the events that followed. On July 20, one of the conspirators, Claus von Stauffenberg, planted a bomb in the so-called "Wolf's Lair", Hitler's headquarters in Rastenburg in Eastern Prussia. But Hitler was only lightly wounded. The simultaneous take-over attempts in Berlin and Paris were quickly subdued by troops loyal to Hitler. The putting down of the coup was followed by a wave of arrests and summary trials. Most of the conspirators were executed immediately after the trial. During the investigation, the notorious German secret police, the Gestapo, learned that Rommel was aware of the plot and that he was to take on an important position within the new government.

But he was not arrested. Hitler was afraid of how people might react to the news that even the most popular German officer was involved in the plot. So Hitler and Field Marshal Wilhelm Keitel decided to offer him an honourable death. If he accepted, they promised not to persecute his family. They would be allowed to keep all their privileges.

On October 14 1944, two high officers visited Rommel who was recuperating at his well-guarded home in Herrlingenu near Ulm. They told him that he could choose between a trial or Hitler's offer for him to commit suicide. Rommel bid farewell to his wife Lucie and his son Manfred. He joined the two officers in the car. They drove into the forest where Rommel drank the poison they had brought. Officially it was announced that Rommel had succumbed to the wounds he had received in an air attack. He was buried in Ulm with full military honours. Lucie and Manfred had to swear they would keep quiet about the real cause of his death. It was Wilhelm Keitel who, during his trial in Nurnberg, revealed to the public the true circumstances of Rommel's death.

Part 2:
ALONG THE PATH OF THE BREACH

SOME INTERESTING STATISTICS

It is general knowledge that young Rommel participated at the breach of the front at Kobarid. But it is less known - in fact quite unknown - just how important his role was in the operation. This episode does not attract even the attention of his biographers. And yes, if it was not for the vicinity of the site, it probably would not interest me either. The lack of attention can clearly be seen in an analysis of Rommel biographies. Without a pictorial appendix, the book by Charles Douglas-Home entitled "Rommel" has 140 pages. Approximately two of them are devoted to the fighting at the Soča (Isonzo) river. That represents approximately 1.5% of the book. 11 pages (approximately 8%) describe "Blitzkrieg" in Poland and France, as many as 76 (approximately 54%) are devoted to the North African campaign and 17 (approximately 12%) to preparations for the invasion and the invasion in Normandy itself. David Irwing's book, "The Trail of the Fox" is similar. Of 600 pages only 8 describe the Soča battle (approximately 1.3%), Poland in 1939 and France in 1940 are covered by 29 (almost 5%), fighting in the desert by 281 (approximately 47%) and preparations of the Atlantic Wall and the Normandy invasion by 131 pages (approximately 22%). The main exception is Rommel's own book "Infantry Attacks" (the original title of which was "Infanterie greift an"), which is devoted entirely to events during the First World War, but being written by

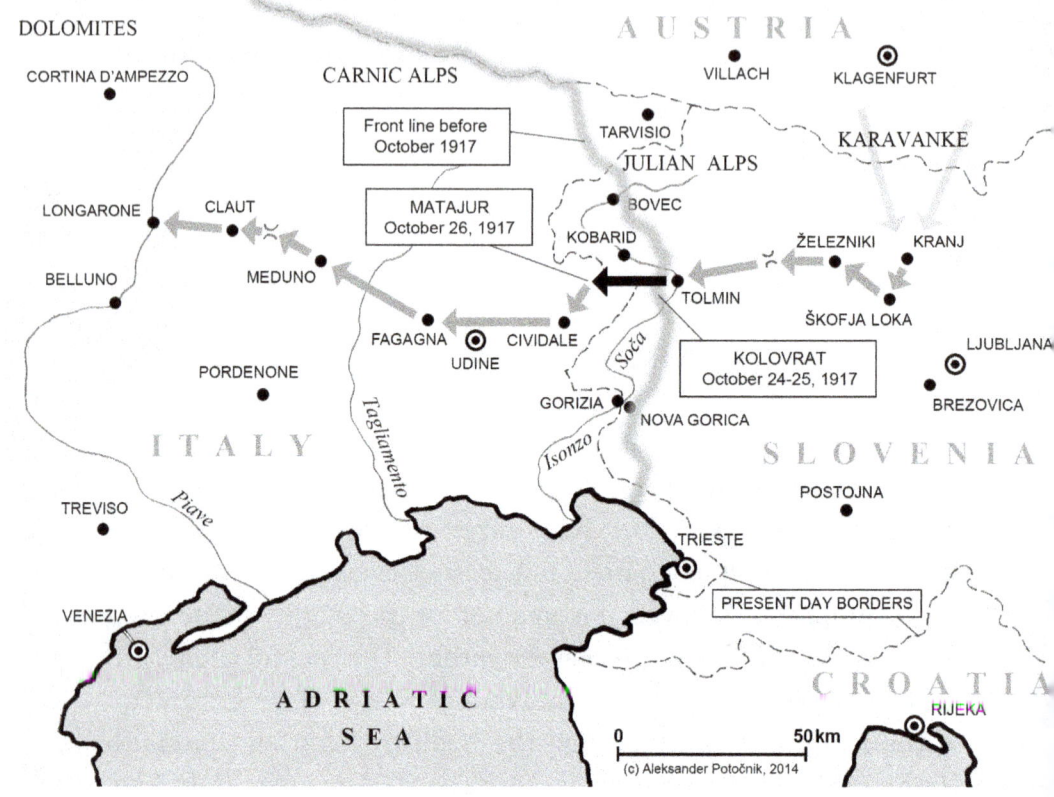

The theatre of the operations and Rommel's movement during October 1917. The darker arrow marks the breach of the front line near Kobarid (Caporetto). Diagram: Aleksander J. Potočnik.

Rommel himself and published in 1937, it can hardly be considered a representative example.

It is on the basis of Rommel's own book that we can determine how very important his role was. True, Rommel did not openly claim, "Without my imaginative manoeuvres the breach would have been achieved with significantly bigger difficulties." or even, "Without my participation the breach would fail." But from his description of events and his comparisons of actions happening at the same time at different locations one arrives at exactly such a conclusion. Of course, we must face the inevitable question, "To what degree can Rommel be trusted?" Was he exaggerating? Considering his skilful and willing cooperation with the German propaganda machine in creating his own myth such a question appears valid. Rommel gladly posed for the cameras, doing it with a notable degree of talent. A great portion of documentary material about him that is available today was either staged or acted. However, quotes by David Irwing, otherwise a controversial historian, but probably the most qualified of Rommel's biographers, speaks in Rommel's favour. His frustration over the fact that another officer received the *Pour le Merite* award speaks about his own awareness of the importance of his actions. On the other hand, the fact that his complaints were noted and that he received the award at the first subsequent occasion, with the explanation that it refers also to the Kobarid breach, demonstrates that others also soon became aware of the significance of his achievement.

To put it in another way, the "Miracle of Caporetto" itself

Left: A cover of Rommel's original book »Infanterie greift an« (a 1942 edition) Source: NUK - National and University Library of Slovenia

Right: The cover of the Slovenian edition containing a chapter about developments in October 1917. Source: Kobarid Museum.

- the advance of the units attacking from Bovec and Tolmin, which met at the village of Srpenica near Kobarid and thus cut off all the Italian troops on the ridges of Polovnik and Krasji Vrh, is not really Rommel's contribution. But breaching the second and the third line of defence and the consequent rapid advance of the Austrian and German armies from the ridges of Kolovrat and Matajur and down the valley of the Nadiža (Natissone) river towards Cividale certainly is. The breach could have succeeded without Rommel, but it would certainly have unfolded at a slower pace and with a much higher number of casualties on both sides. We can therefore conclude with a sufficient degree of certainty that Rommel's actions, considering their vast consequences, have not really been given enough attention.

THE ROAD TO THE ISONZO FRONT

During the Kobarid operation, The Alpine Corps, part of which was Rommel's WGB, was to function as the left flank of the German 12th Division. Thanks to the photographic material collected by Mr Marko Štepec, a custodian of the Museum of Contemporary History of Slovenia, we can easily reconstruct the path of that Division to the front. Its units were first ferried by train from Colmar in Alsace via Augsburg, Jesenice and Ljubljana to the encampment near the village of Brezovica, ten kilometres south of Ljubljana. From Brezovica they continued their way on foot to the towns of Škofja Loka and Železniki and then via Petrovo Brdo pass to Podbrdo. Down the gorge of the Bača, they finally reached the valley of the Soča (Isonzo) river.

Unlike the 12th Division, Rommel's soldiers travelled mainly at night and could not take photographs, so there is no photographic documentation left by them. But since from

Above: German troops passing Škofja Loka on their way to the Soča/Isonzo valley. Source: National Museum of Contemporary History of Slovenia.

Below: The view of Škofja Loka today, taken from a similar spot. The area from which the original photo was taken is today completely built up. Photo: author.

Above: Austrian and German troops on their march up the Selška Sora river valley. Source: National Museum of Contemporary History of Slovenia.

Below: Remnants of iron smelter in the town of Železniki are a modest reminder of the once intensive iron production in the Selška Sora river valley. Photo: author.

Škofja Loka onwards, the WGB's trail matches that of the 12th Division, the archive material of the 12th division represents a precious documentation of the conditions of Rommel's own travel.

The main difference between the journey of 12th Division and that of the WGB is that Rommel's unit did not detour via Ljubljana and Brezovica. Rommel himself writes, "Early in October I resumed command of my detachment. We were located in beautiful Carinthia to which the battalion had been sent via Macedonia." And after explaining the aim of the operation he continues, "With night marches and braving heavy rain we conquered the ridge of Karavanke, a total distance of about 100 kilometres." This quote and especially the word "conquered" suggests that the soldiers of the WGB walked either over Ljubelj Pass (Loiblpass) or Jezersko Pass (Seebergsattel). The place of assembly before the last leg of the journey was the city of Kranj.

On October 18th, the battalion set off towards the front. From here on, Rommel's description of the journey is quite meticulous: Kranj, Škofja loka, Zali Log, Podbrdo and finally Kneža which Rommel's detachment reached on October 21. They needed three days for this relatively short journey since they were able to travel only during the night. During the day they had to encamp and camouflage their lodgings well so that enemy aviators would not notice the approach of the troops gathering for the offensive.

Back in the seventies, I believe it was in 1978, I scouted a trail with a good friend of mine, Zoran Daljević, for an orientation competition. Just under the Petrovo Brdo Pass, a farmer allowed us to stay overnight in a barn. In the morning, a friendly local came to greet us. During the conversation he pointed to the imposing farmhouse. "You see this house? During the First World War Erwin Rommel spent a week here in this very house, before departing for the Soča valley. Surely you've heard of him? He was a German officer and later, in the Second World War, became known as the Desert Fox." Since, even then, we knew about Rommel, we believed the man. But it was only when I began to prepare this book, that I realised I had not asked him for his name. When I started to prepare the book I suddenly regretted this failure since I was sure that after all these years such a little piece of local tradition was lost.

So now, almost three decades later, I returned to the Petrovo Brdo Pass, accompanied by photographer Rafael Marn. We stopped at the little coffee house that was erected a few years ago at the top of the saddle. We were greeted by a friendly innkeeper with an unbeatable broad smile. Mr Rudolf Zgaga, the innkeeper, had a busy day. Sunny weather had attracted numerous bikers and cyclists who stopped at his hut and he went around serving them all with equal attention

The house of Rudolf Zgaga, a very likely lodging place of Rommel's on the Petrovo Brdo Pass. Photo: author.

and bestowing his broad, friendly smile on all of them. We had a cup of coffee and, despite his obligations, Mr Zgaga found a couple of minutes to talk to us. I asked him if he had ever heard a story about Rommel being here. "Of course! " he replied, "He stayed in our house and my great aunt kept him company! She kept retelling the experience till the day she died." He paused for a second, "Wait, I can show you a photo. "

My own smile must have matched that of Rudolf Zgaga.

Left: A photo of a group of German officers standing on the overpass atop the Petrovo Brdo pass. According to Mr Rudolf Zgaga one of them is Erwin Rommel. Curtesy of Rudolf Zgaga.

Right: the same overpass at the top of the Petrovo Brdo pass with Mr Rudolf Zgaga and the author. Photo: Rafael Marn.

Above: Mr Rudolf Zgaga related an interesting story about Erwin Rommel, the field-marshal-to-be, staying on their estate and socialising with his then teenage great-aunt Alojzija Zgaga. Photo: Rafael Marn.

Below: The Zgaga family home photographed shortly before the First World War. Courtesy of Rudolf Zgaga, reproduction by Rafael Marn.

Above: German troops descending to Podbrdo, a township below the Petrovo Brdo pass. Courtesy of Rudolf Zgaga, reproduction by Rafael Marn.

Above: This intersection with a railway line entering the tunnel at Hudajužna was one of the bottlenecks in the gorge of the Bača River. Courtesy of the National Museum of Contemporary History of Slovenia.

Below: A road tunnel has been constructed recently to avoid the former bottleneck. Photo: author.

Above: The village of Kneža was WGB's last encampment before departing to the position on the northern slope of Bučenica. Photo: author.

Below: To depart from Kneža Rommel and the WGB had no choice but to use this old bridge, now used only by the locals. Photo: author.

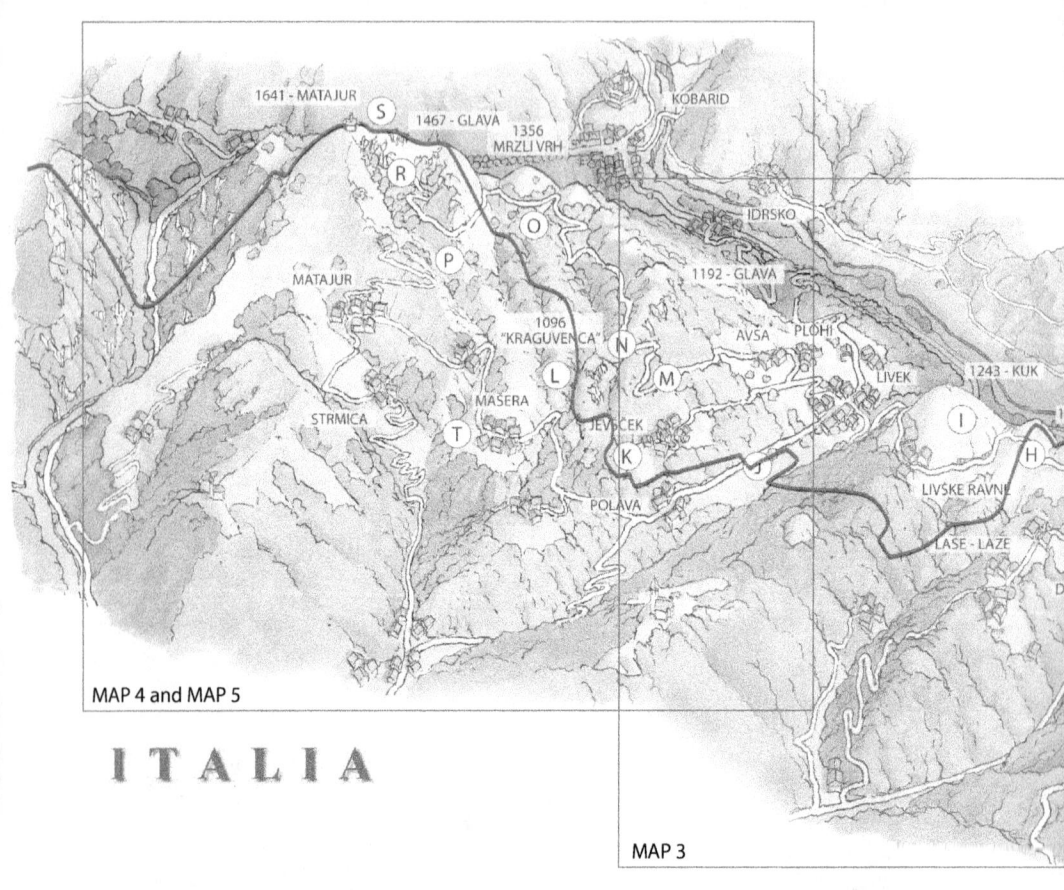

An overview map of the activities of Rommel's detachment from 23rd to 26th of October 1917 (a view from the south towards the north).

MAP 1 (October 23, 1917)

The approach of Rommel and the WGB from Kneža to their starting point at Bučenica (A)

MAP 2 (October 24, 1917)

A - Starting point at the northern slope of Bučenica. The infantry attack starts at 8.00 a.m.

B - Rommel's detachment, acting as the right flank of the Leib Regiment, breaches the first Italian line near the church of St Daniel and reaches the foot of Mount Hlevnik.

C – Italians defending the second line stop Rommel's advance.

D – Rommel retreats and climbs up the gorge. He conquers the second Italian line by stealth.

E – Once the way is freed for the Leib regiment to advance, Rommel's detachment clears the slopes of Mt Hlevnik and retires for the night.

MAP 3 (October 25, 1917)

F – In the morning the Leib Regiment attacks the Quote 1114 (Na Gradu) but manages to capture only part of the peak.

G – Rommel's detachment follows the ridge of Kolovrat, finds a weak point and breaches the third Italian line.

H – Under the rise called Nagnoj Italians block Rommel's advance. Rommel conquers it after a rather elaborate manoeuvre.

I – During the intensive shelling of Mt Kuk Rommel's detachment circumvents it and following the ridge road reaches the village of Livške Ravne.

J – Rommel's detachment descends into the valley and on the road Livek – Polava captures the 4th Bersaglieri Brigade.

SLOVENIA

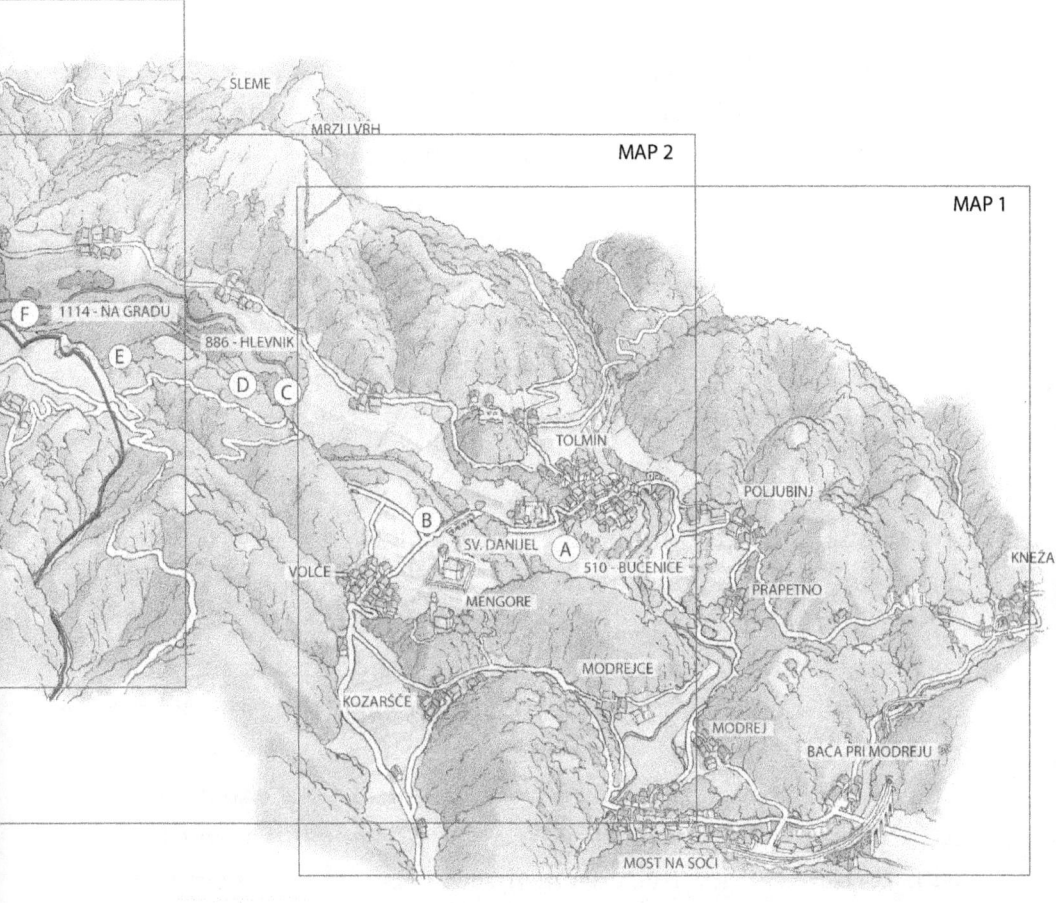

K – Rommel's detachment climbs to the village of Jevšček.

MAP 4 and MAP 5 (October 26, 1917)

L – At 5 a.m. Rommel's attachment attacks Mt Kraguvenca, but is repulsed.

M – Rommel turns and from behind attacks the Italian defensive line above Jevšček. Italian defenders surrender.

N – Reinforced with the crew left in Jevšček Rommel again attacks Mt Kraguvenca and captures it.

O – Under the peak of Mrzli vrh the 1st Regiment of the Salerno Brigade surrenders to Rommel's detachment.

P – Rommel's detachment circumvents Italian positions on Mt Glava (Quote 1467).

R – Under Mt Matajur the 2nd Regiment of the Salerno Brigade surrenders to Rommel's detachment.

S – The crew at the peak of Mt Matajur at first puts up some resistance, but surrenders at 11.40 a.m.

The red (dark) line on the picture indicates the present day national border between Italy and Slovenia.

Trivia: During the three day operation, Rommel crossed the future border line at least eleven times.

PREPARATIONS FOR THE OFFENSIVE

On October 21, Rommel joined the commander of the WGB, Major Sprösser for the reconnaissance of the slope of the Bučenica Hill which was to be the starting point of their attack. The task of settling the 11 companies of the battalion on the slope in plain view of the enemy and hiding them on the scree and in the gorges seemed virtually impossible. But the concentration of troops in the area was so high that there was no other possibility. During the night of October 22nd, WGB soldiers moved to the allotted position, dug in and camouflaged themselves.

From Rommel's notes we know which route from Kneža to Bučenica the reconnaissance party followed. They took the Bača gorge to the congruence of the Bača and Idrijca Rivers where a magnificent railway bridge spans the valley. From there they went to Most na Soči, a village then known as Sveta Lucija and nowadays famous for its archaeological findings, crossed the Soča river and climbed up the southern slope of Bučenica, where the Italians were unable to see them. But did the entire WGB use the same route? We cannot say that with certainty since there were three possibilities. Apart from the route of the reconnaissance party, they could have used the ancient merchant road called "The Old Celtica" which climbs uphill from Kneža, through the villages of Podmelec and Ljubinj, over the Hum Pass and reaches the Soča valley at Tolmin. This route was used to supply the battlefield north of Tolmin, most notably the Mrzli Vrh peak. The former importance of this route, which is now only a narrow local road, was recognised by the builders of the Vallo Alpino defence line who in the 1930s constructed a fort at the Hum Pass. But the notion that this route was used by the WGB to reach Bučenica did not seem to me to be very likely until I learnt about a pontoon bridge, which the Austrians built near a river bend called Pod Ključem. It makes the journey along the "Old Celtica" plausible.

There was another possible route of approach. Following the Bača river, the troops could have, after the congruence with the Idrijca River, turned towards the village of Modrej rather than to Most na Soči. This would again bring them to the pontoon bridge at Pod Ključem. Unfortunately, Rommel's short note, "We had to leave our pack animals at the eastern slope of Bučenica", does not give enough detail to conclude which of the three routes his soldiers took.

In the summers of 2011 and 2012, I had a chance to participate in the preparation and execution of the first serious archaeological research of the Soča/Isonzo Front, conducted by a joint team of archaeologists from the Slovenian Institute for the Protection of Cultural Heritage and from Bristol University in Great Britain. The research was carried out on the western slope of Bučenica and Mengore. A small group of us decided to follow the trench lines leading horizontally towards the northern slope of Bučenica. On the spot where the western slope sharply breaks into the northern one, the trenches stopped. Clearly the defenders deemed the slope impassable and therefore saw no need to fortify it. Yet, in October 1917, this very northern slope was allotted to Rommel's WGB as the starting point for their action.

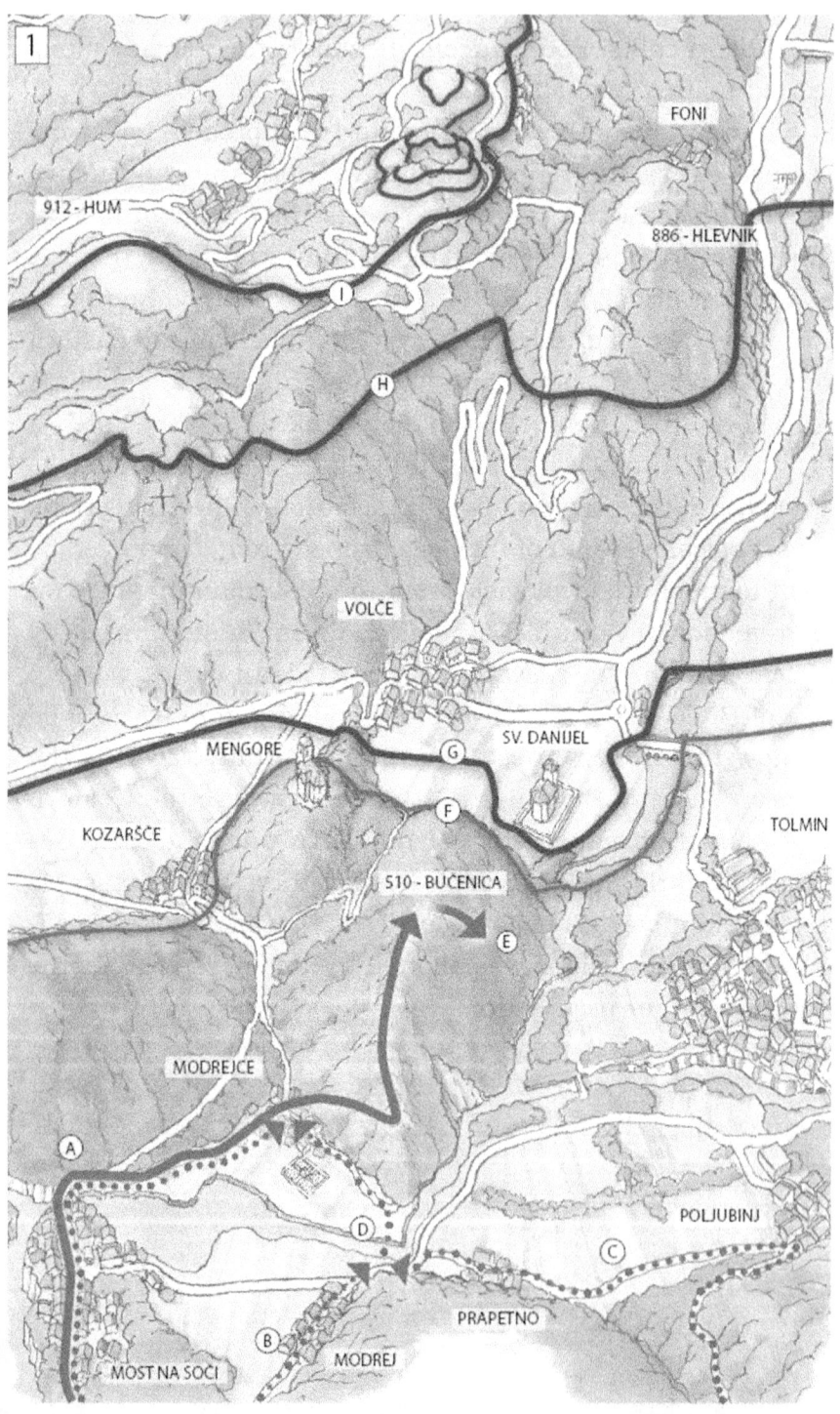

Map 1, showing the approach of the WGB to the front line (views from the east and from the south - illustrations by the author). The full line indicates the route taken by the officers of the WGB when on reconnaissance on October 21. Dotted lines indicate two other possible routes that the soldiers of the WGB could have taken in the night between October 22 and 23.

A – Most na Soči (St Lucia).

B – A route through Modrej.

C – A route following the "Old Celtica" via Hum.

D – The site of the pontoon bridge.

E – WGB's starting point on the slope of Mt Bučenica.

F – Austrian line.

G – The first Italian line.

H – The second Italian line.

I – The third Italian line.

Above: The crossroads by the old church in Kneža. The modern road passes along the left hand side of the church while the "Old Celtica" climbs the hill along its right flank. We know with certainty that a day earlier, when on a reconnaissance, Rommel took the left road, but when returning with the entire WGB he could have taken either. Photo: author.

Below: German heavy artillery arriving at the front line. Courtesy of the National Museum of Contemporary History of Slovenia.

The troops that took the left, modern road via Bača pri Modreju and Most na Soči (then Santa Lucia) passed by a picturesque railway bridge.

Above: German troops arriving in Bača pri Modreju in October 1917. Courtesy of Florjan Pirih.

Below left: The most famous picture of the Bača pri Modreju bridge is that showing Archduke Karl - the future Austro-Hungarian Emperor Karl I inspecting Austrian troops in 1916. Courtesy of Branko Drekonja.

Below right: The Bača pri Modreju bridge today, as seen from a passing train. Photo: author.

Above: Austro - German troops at the picturesque saddle of Hum. The troops taking the "Old Celtica" road had to use this passage, later a site of a Vallo Alpino fort. Courtesy of the National Museum of Contemporary History of Slovenia.

Below: The same road today. Photo: author.

Above: German soldiers on the "Old Celtica" road over Hum. Courtesy of the National Museum of Contemporary History of Slovenia.

Below: The dark mass on the left is the northern slope of Bučenica, the starting position of the WGB. The rise on the right is Hlevnik, just beyond it is Quote 1114 - na Gradu. Photo: author.

THE FIRST DAY - OCTOBER 24, 1917

The twelfth Isonzo Battle started on 24 October, 1917 at 2 o'clock in the morning with fierce artillery shelling of the Italian positions behind the first defensive line, the main target being the artillery batteries. The surprise was complete and Rommel speaks of his relief over the lack of response from the Italians. Rommel's soldiers observed the bombardment for a while and then returned to their shelters to catch some more rest. In the morning the shelling started with new ferocity, but now it was directed at the Italian first line. The aim was to destroy barbed wire and other obstacles to make the approach of the infantry as easy as possible.

It was raining when the battalion left its position on the slope of Bučenica and moved along the river bank towards the line in the direction of the village of Volče. Higher on the slope, the Bavarian Infantry Regiment Leib was also descending towards the front line. The task of the Leib Regiment was to breach the defences on Kolovrat advancing along the line Mount Hlevnik – Na Gradu (Quote 1114). Rommel's WGB was to defend the Leib's right flank on the northern slopes of Hlevnik and neutralise Italian artillery positions around the settlement of Foni. As we shall see, Rommel very soon surpassed his "mandate".

At 8 o'clock, the artillery fire moved ahead and the infantry surged forward. Rommel's detachment was advancing from the foot of Bučenica towards the church of St Daniel and the first Italian line. Surviving Italian defenders in trenches around the church surrendered the moment they sighted the first German soldiers. Despite some weak machine gun fire from the peaks around them, the soldiers of the Leib Regiment and the WGB ran over the plain between Bučenica and Hlevnik. The Leib Regiment attacked Hlevnik frontally, up the eastern slope. Meanwhile WGB advanced along the northern slope of Hlevnik, which offered some shelter from Italian machine gun fire. They used a path that today still ascends from Volče towards Foni.

All of a sudden, the point of the WGB column was stopped by intensive machine gun fire. They had reached the second Italian defensive line. Rommel quickly realised that charging positions ahead would demand heavy casualties. He decided to bypass them instead. He remembered that a little earlier they had passed a gorge and he decided to use it. He left a part of his unit at the path to Foni to keep the Italians busy and to hide his own movements. He then returned with the rest of the detachment and started to climb up the gorge. At the edge of the forest, they noticed Italian units untouched by the artillery fire. The attention of the Italians was directed upwards towards the ridge where the sound of battle could be heard. From the noise of the battle, Rommel concluded that the attack of the Leib Regiment had stalled. Hoping to achieve a surprise, he organised his detachment for an attack,

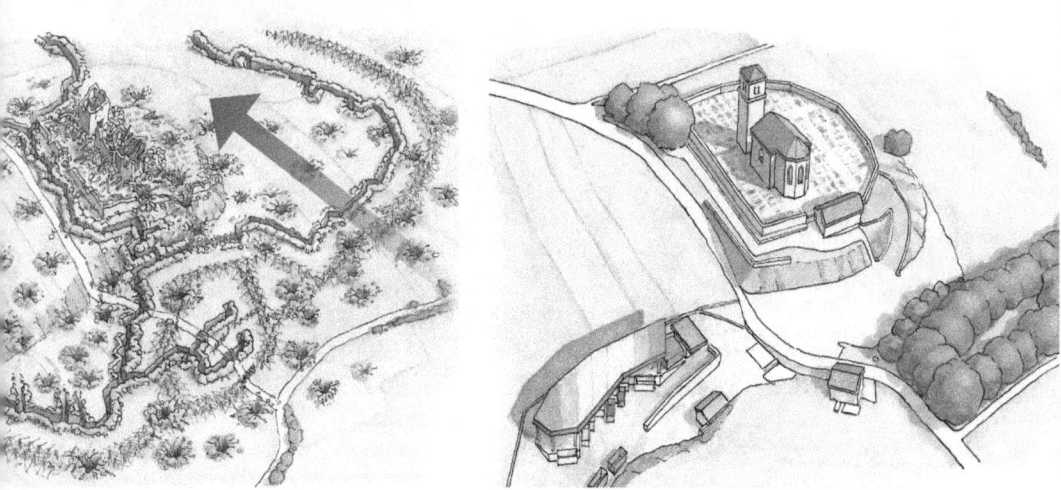

The church of St Daniel as part of the Italian line (left) and today (right). Arrow indicates the direction of Rommel's advance. Drawings by the author.

Above: A view of Bučenica from Hlevnik. Two thin white arrows indicate the advance of Rommel's unit. The yellow line denotes the direction of advance of the Leib Regiment. The church of St Daniel was a part of the first Italian line. Photo: author.

Below: Captured defenders of the first Italian defence line. Source: Europeana Collections 1914-1918, stored by the Bildarchiv Austria.

but then he spotted a well-camouflaged military supply path coming up from the direction of Volče. Because of the rain and the camouflage, visibility was limited and the Italians might easily assume that a group coming up the path in a leisurely way were their own soldiers. He explained his idea to Corporal Kiefner and charged him with choosing a couple of men. Soon a group of soldiers appeared on the path and slowly moved upwards. There were some long minutes to wait before one of Kiefner's soldiers returned to report that the plan had succeeded. Without firing a single shot, Kiefner's group had seized a machine gun garrison of 17 men guarding the passage. A three company strong detachment now rushed into the opening and secured it by occupying the trenches fifty metres above and below the passage. By doing so, Rommel's detachment breached the second Italian defence line – without firing a single shot.

It soon became clear that the enemy had not noticed what had happened. So Rommel decided to abandon the original plan and exploit the situation in the most efficient way possible. Since his instructions stated, "Without limiting the day's activity in space and time, continue the advance to the west, knowing that we have strong reserves with and behind us", he opted to neglect his contacts with the units to his left and right. Rather than continuing along the slope, he decided to take the ridge of Hlevnik and then attack the main body of defenders on the northern slope from above.

Encountering many isolated enemy posts, Rommel's soldiers neutralised them by bypassing them and surprising them from behind. All this passed without shooting, which enabled Rommel to maintain the element of surprise. The biggest problem represented German artillery fire. He couldn't warn the German gunners without betraying their advance. Luckily, only one soldier was wounded - by a stone that was dislodged when a German shell exploded.

After taking two Italian artillery batteries, Rommel's soldiers reached the ridge where they encountered some of the Lieb Regiment soldiers. They continued together towards the peak of Hlevnik which was under heavy artillery fire. "While the Leibers sat down, waiting for the artillery fire to move forwards," wrote Rommel, "I led my company to the northern slope of Hlevnik." In this way, without encountering any resistance, Rommel outflanked the Italian defences, reached the peak of Hlevnik and made the crew his prisoners. Realising that the peak had fallen, the Italian gunners started to fire on them, so Rommel's detachment retreated to the northern slope again. Now Rommel ordered his soldiers to carry out their original task of neutralising artillery positions between Hlevnik and Foni. They took 17 cannons, of which 12 were of "heavy calibre". We can assume these were the renowned "149s".

At 15.30, Rommel was informed that the main body of the Leib Regiment had arrived at the saddle between Hlevnik and quote 1114. As Quote 1114 Rommel marked a rise called Na Gradu, a part of the Kolovrat ridge that represented a key stronghold of the Italian third defensive line. As the Leib regiment began his advance towards Quote 1114, Rommel's detachment resumed the role of the right flank. His units "cleaned up" the area around Quote 1066. At dusk, Rommel observed some attempts by the Leib's 3rd battalion to conquer Quote 1114. The attack failed and everybody present was of the opinion that the rise could not be defeated without an introductory heavy artillery barrage. Night fell and after a few more futile attempts to advance further towards Quote 1114, all the German units concluded their activities.

At 19.00, an interesting event occurred. Rommel was summoned by the commander of the Leib Regiment, Major Count Bothmer. He demanded that Rommel submit himself to his command. Rommel strongly declined the possibility, stating

The fortified positions at the Quote 1114 - Na Gradu are preserved as an oper-air museum. Photo: author.

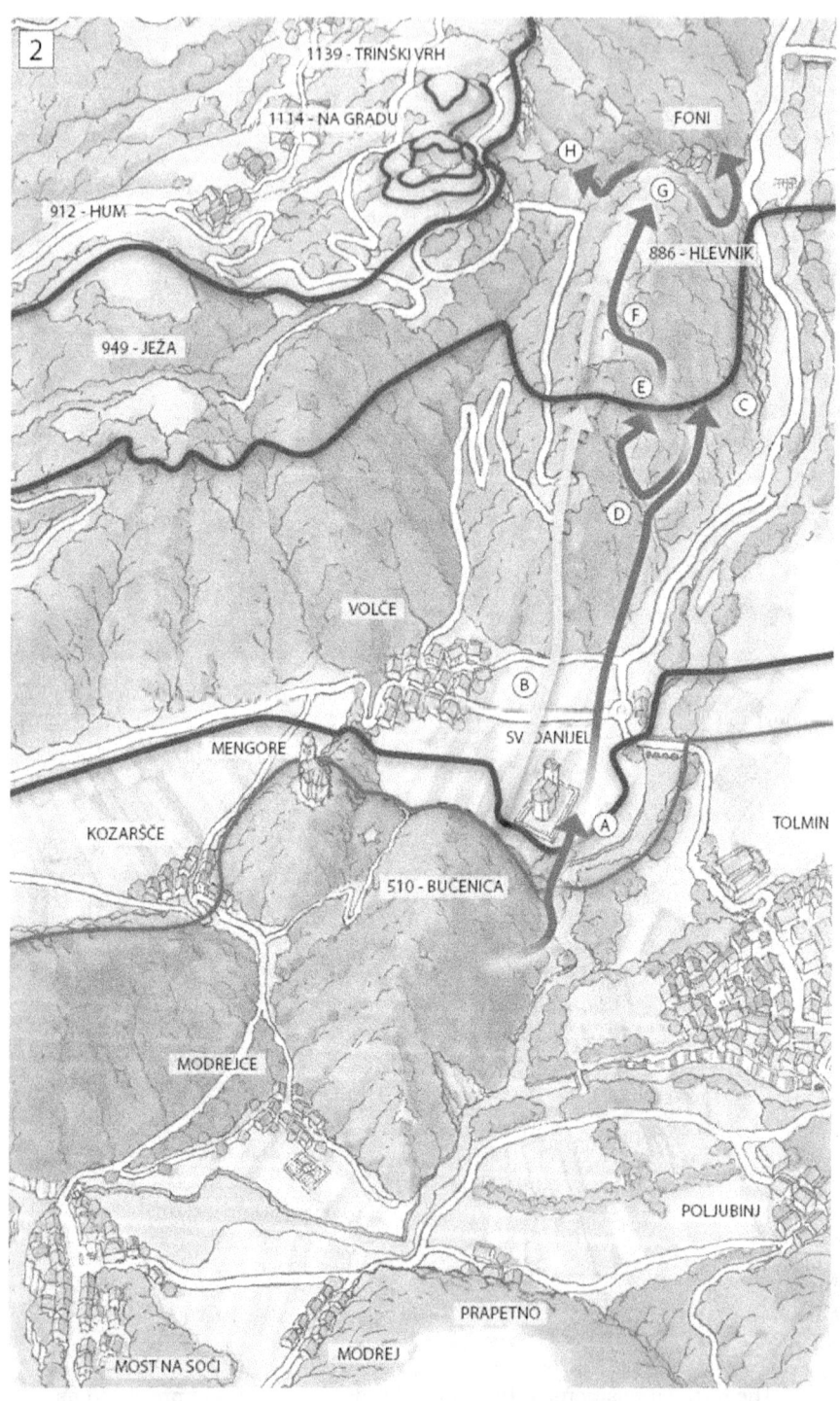

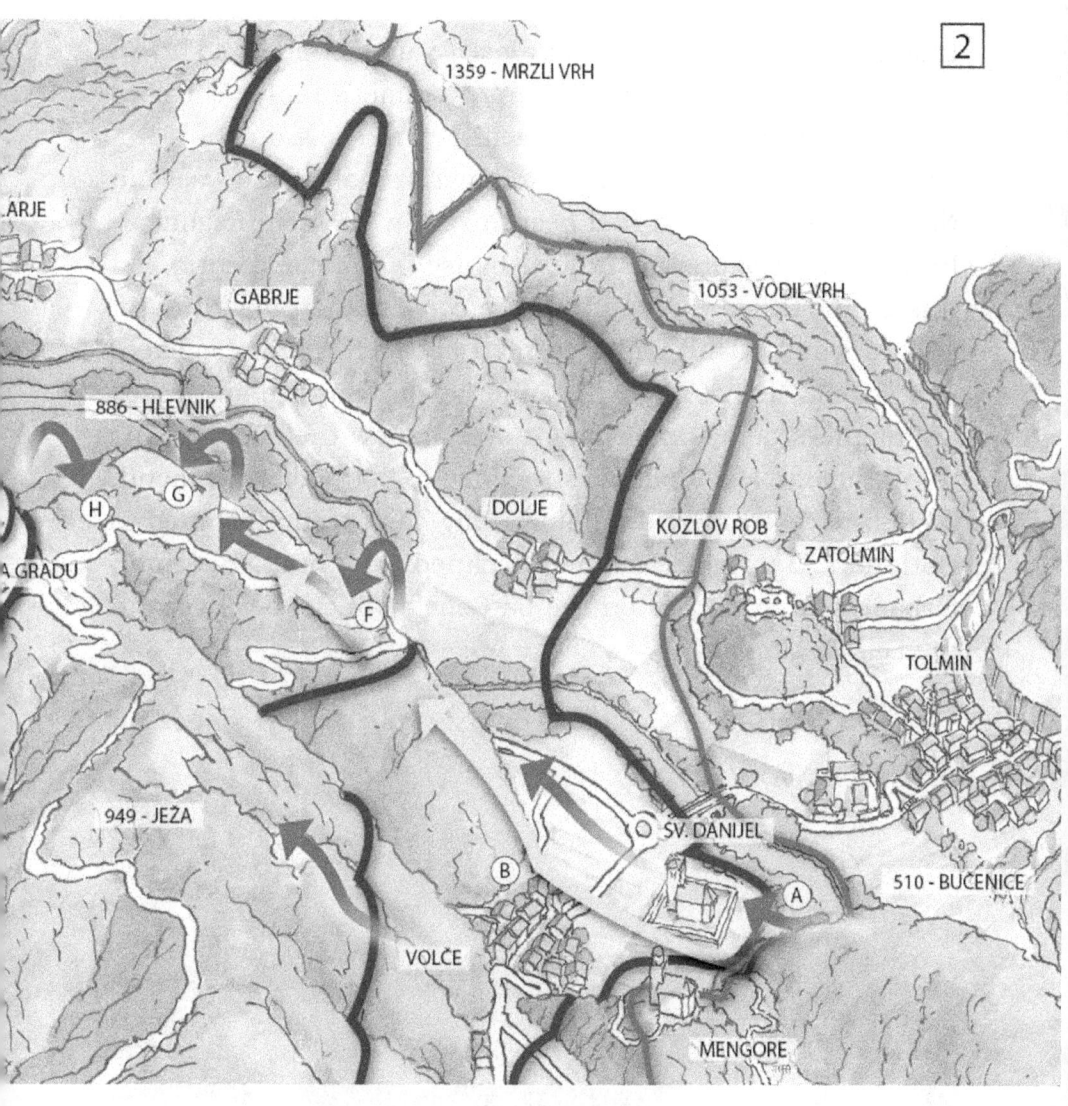

Map 2, showing the operations during the first day of the breach, October 24, 1917 (views from the east and from the south - illustrations by the author).

A – Rommel's detachment breaches the first Italian line at the church of St Daniel.

B – The Leib Regiment breaches the front near Volče and advances up the ridge of Mt Hlevnik.

C – Rommel stopped at the Italian second line.

D – Rommel's attachment climbs the gorge and surprises the Italians.

E – Rommel captures the second line without firing a shot.

F – Rommel's detachment reaches the ridge of Mt Hlevnik and opens the way for the Lieb Regiment.

G – Rommel's detachment reaches the peak of Mt Hlevnik.

H – Rommel's detachment encamps for the night under the Quote 1066.

that his commander, Major Sprösser, was just about to arrive at their present position. Hearing Rommel's reply, Bothmer forbade him any activity in the direction of Quote 1114 Na Gradu or westwards from it. Rommel was allowed to ascend Na Gradu only once it had been taken by the Leib Regiment. In his book, Rommel restrained himself from commenting on this event. But the account of the conversation is written in such a way that it is easy to read between the lines. There is a strong hint of Major Bothmer's fear that the successes of Rommel's detachment might overshadow the efforts of his own regiment. Had Rommel submitted to Bothmer's command, all his successes would automatically have been attributed to Bothman. But since Rommel declined to submit, Bothman forbade him to appear on the battlefield which "belonged" to the Leib Regiment.

As the first day ended the peak of the Quote 1114 - Na Gradu was still firmly held by the Italians. Photo: author.

THE SECOND DAY – OCTOBER 25, 1917

During the night, Rommel, reflected on Bothmer's order and found it hard to accept. He believed that even with strong artillery support the frontal attack on the fortified positions of Na Gradu could not succeed without huge losses. He judged that it would be far better to surprise the Italian defenders with a sudden attack further westwards along the Kolovrat ridge. At 5 am, while it was still dark, Major Sprösser arrived at Quote 1066. Rommel reported to him the demand made by Major Bothmer. He also described his idea to try to go further west from Quote 1114 – Na Gradu. He asked for four companies of mountain hunters and one machine gun company. The Major agreed to the proposed action but allowed Rommel only two companies of mountain hunters and a machinegun company, promising to send more if Rommel's attempt proved successful.

Rommel set off along the slope of Kolovrat about two hundred metres under the top of the ridge. While advancing, he was listening to the noise from Quote 1114. Rommel's detachment kept a low profile, hoping that the soldiers in the fortified line running along the crest of the ridge would not spot them. After a prolonged and careful advance they covered a distance of about two kilometres. Suddenly his soldiers surprised and disarmed the Italian Advanced Post guarding a gully. The Italians were observing the advance of the German 12th and Austro-Hungarian 50th Divisions along the valley below and paid no attention to the slope on their right. This gave Rommel an opportunity to use the gully for a stealth approach to the Italian main line. He phoned Major Sprösser to inform him of his decision. From Major Sprösser he found out that the Leib Regiment had failed to attack Na Gradu since the Italians conducted a counter attack first.

Rommel sent up a reconnaissance party. Meanwhile

Italian fortified positions along the Kolovrat ridge. The Soča river can be seen in the valley. The slope along which Rommel's detachment was searching for an Italian weak spot is seen between the ridge and the river valley. Photo: author.

his detachment assembled in the gully and Rommel was worried about the high concentration of his soldiers. Then a report came that the reconnaissance party managed to cross the obstacles and surprise the defenders at their morning ablutions. Rommel and his detachment ran uphill, jumped over the obstacle and found themselves in enemy trenches. On the other side of the saddle, they reached an Italian-built camouflaged mountain road following the crest on the safe, southern side. Soon the entire German detachment was on the saddle while the Italians to the left and to the right along the ridge had still not noticed anything.

Rommel knew that he might have just conquered the last Italian line, but all depended on managing to secure his achievement. He gave a machine gun platoon under Sargent Spadinger the charge to secure the ridge towards the east – the direction of Quote 1114 – Na Gradu. He then sent Lieutenant Ludwig with the 2nd company to clear the defence line along

The site of the breach seen from Slovenian (above) and Italian (below) side of the present day border. Photo: author.

the ridge towards the west. He commanded the remaining forces himself. He followed the mountain road to the west, hoping to intercept any Italian reserves before they could organise a counter attack. All went well until they reached Quote 1192, a rise called Nagnoj. Rommel's advance was blocked by heavy machine gun fire. Ludwig's 2nd company on the northern side of the ridge fared even worse. They found themselves trapped between Italian reserves and high barbed wire obstacles. Luckily, the 2nd company was advancing along the trench which now provided some good cover. But they could not move and the Italian superiority was becoming more and more obvious.

Rommel reacted swiftly. He left a small unit to keep engaging the enemy and, hidden by the camouflage above the road, returned with his troops to the saddle where they had breached the line. From here they followed the trail of the 2nd company along the trenches, but shortly before reaching the battleground Rommel ascended to a knoll above the trenches. This gave him an opportunity to observe the situation. The Italians were advancing towards the 2nd company, exposing their left flank to Rommel, who ordered his unit to charge. The second company realised what was happening and made a counter-attack as well. Realising that they had been attacked from two sides, the Italians surrendered. Only the officers tried to keep firing and Rommel wrote, "I had to interfere to save them from the fury of mountain soldiers." About 500 soldiers and 12 officers were caught and the way to the peak of Nagnoj was wide open. But Rommel was saddened by his own loss. One of the two of his fallen soldiers was brave Corporal Kiefner who had, just a day before, penetrated the second defence line at the slope of Hlevnik.

From the top of Nagnoj, Rommel observed the movement of Italian troops towards Quote 1114. He was even more worried about the Italians who gathered on the 1243 metre high Mount Kuk, the last peak at the western end of the Kolovrat ridge. But the Italian commander gave him an unexpected present. Rather than counter-attacking he ordered his troops to dig in on the eastern slope of Kuk facing Nagnoj. This gave Rommel enough time to consolidate his gains and regroup his forces.

At 10.30, Major Sprösser, his staff and the remaining parts of the WGB arrived at Nagnoj. They were followed by elements of the Leib regiment who had taken the Quote 1114

 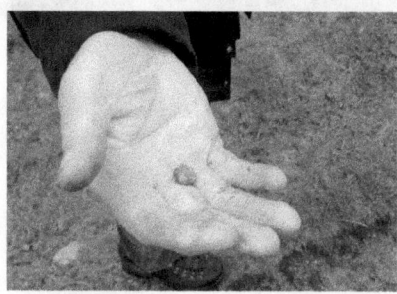

Above: The peak of Nagnoj. Observe the road and the diagonal trench and consequent obvious similarity with the illustration described in the introduction.

Below: A shrapnel picked up on the Nagnoj battlefield. Photos: author.

itself, but not the part of the ridge between Quote 1114 and Rommel's detachment. Meanwhile Rommel had managed to get in touch with one of the German batteries in the valley. By 11.00, the preparations for the attack on Kuk were completed. At 11.15 the German battery opened fire on the new Italian positions on the eastern slope of Kuk. A duel ensued between the Italian and the German machine gunners. But the attack directly from Nagnoj towards Kuk was just a trick. Rommel's own detachment was to attack the peak from the south.

Just before setting off, Rommel learned that some

Above: Mt Kuk with the road that Rommel used to circumvent the Italian positions on Mt Kuk and reach Livške Ravne. Photo: author.

Below: The same road leading to the village of Livške Ravne. A few houses can be seen on the slope in the background. The rise behind the village is "Mali Vrh" or Na Muzce. Photo: author.

Leib Regiment units were assigned to the attack on Kuk as well. This gave Rommel a new idea. Knowing that the fate of the Kuk garrison was now sealed he decided to use the Italian mountain road, descending Kuk's southern slope towards a settlement of Livške Ravne to outflank the hill of Kuk completely. He quickly explained the idea to his men and they rushed down along the road, hurrying as much as their heavy equipment would permit them. On their way they met and disarmed groups of surprised and terrified Italian soldiers. At midday they reached Ravne. The surprised Italian crew scattered in panic. Rommel climbed "Mali Vrh"(5) east of Livške Ravne and looked around. He believed that there was no need any more for him to attack Kuk. Below him, in a valley separating the mountains of Kolovrat and Matajur was the village of Livek. Some fighting was heard north of Livek - the German 12th Division fighting Italian defenders. The prospect of attacking Livek from above and opening the path for the 12th Division was tempting. But Rommel judged such an endeavour too dangerous. If the enemy reacted in time and put up a proper defence he would suffer great losses. Instead, he decided to descend to the village of Polava and cut off all the Italian forces at Livek. Even though all of his troops had not yet gathered, he started to descend into the valley while trying to avoid alarming the Italian garrison on the nearby 956 metre high peak of Škarje. At 12.30, his group reached the valley road 2 kilometres south of Livek, cut the telephone lines and lay in ambush along both sides of the road.

Rommel soon realised that during the advance, contact had been broken and most of his units had failed to follow him. That meant that his forces were insufficient for further advance. Meanwhile – to his great surprise – traffic restarted along the road. His soldiers kept capturing enemy supply trains and groups of soldiers and disarming them without

---

(5) Probably the rise called Na Muzce, elevation 1077 m.

Mt Kuk seen from the opposite, western side. Rommel's detachment descended down this slope into the valley below to cut Italian communication along the road Livek - Polava. Photo: author.

a shot. "Everybody was having fun," wrote Rommel. "Soon we were having trouble handling all the traffic. Business was booming," Among those captured was a group of Italian officers in a staff automobile, who drove along the road to find out why the telephones were not working.

After an hour Rommel's reinforcement were still nowhere to be seen. Instead a large Italian column approached from the direction of Livek. Rommel organised an ambush and sent Officer Candidate Stahl to call on the Italians to surrender. The Italians declined, arrested Stahl and opened fire. Even though Rommel's troops were few, they were well placed and well armed. Besides, one more company joined him during the conflict. After about half an hour, the Italians gave up the fight. 2000 men and 50 officers were captured.

Now Rommel used the captured car to drive to Livek to check the situation there. He arrived at the moment when the WGB and parts of the Lieb Regiment were taking over the village. Knowing that the road from Livek towards the

German officers posing with their booty. This could easily be the car captured by Rommel between Livek and Polava. Courtesy of the National Museum of Contemporary History of Slovenia.

south was blocked, the Italians moved up the mountain road northwards towards Mount Matajur. Rommel met Sprösser. They agreed that following the enemy up the road would be too dangerous. Instead Rommel suggested that he could ascend from his roadblock near Polava to the village of Jevšček and from there to the peak of Kraguvenca (6). That would mean cutting the only road to Matajur and trapping all the Italian forces on Mrzli vrh and Matajur. The Major approved his plan and gave him the necessary units.

It was already dusk when Rommel and his soldiers reached Jevšček. On the way, they circumvented some Italian positions. His advanced party brought the news that Jevšček was fortified, but the positions were still unoccupied. As they approached, they heard some Italian troops heading in the same direction. The Italians occupied the empty trenches above the village and clashed with the head of Rommel's advancing column which managed to keep them out of the village. This

---

(6) In his own book Rommel mistook Mt Strmola for Mt Kraguvenca.

Above: Mr Stane Šekli on one of the Italian fortified positions below the village of Jevšček. The positions were unoccupied which enabled Rommel to enter the village. Photo: author.

Below: the southern approach to the village where a stray mule almost betrayed Rommel's advance to the Italians above the village. Photo: author.

enabled Rommel's detachment to enjoy the hospitality of the locals who made them feel very welcome. According to a local, Mr Leopold Šekli, Rommel asked to speak to someone about the situation. The only person who could speak other languages, including German, was a young orphan girl, Ivana Šekli, who was helping in a nearby inn. Ivana accompanied Rommel to a briefing with his officers which was held in the Brgolič house at the northern end of the village. Their host was Mrs Marija Šekli, who was locally known by the house name Marija Brgolič, and although their surnames were the same, Marija and Ivana were, in fact, not related.

As Ivana Šekli later recalled to her son Alojz, who in turn told the story to Mr Leopold Šekli, one petrol lamp didn't suffice. Rommel demanded more light and Mrs Marija Šekli (Brgolič) had to bring candles too. Ivana gave Rommel a very detailed report about the Italian positions and an Italian deserter gave some valuable information as well. Ivana apparently also advised Rommel not to advance straight on from the village where the noise of his men's footsteps on the stony trail could betray movement of the detachment to the Italians. So Rommel opted to advance to the left of the village. After the briefing, Rommel retired for the night with a good enough knowledge of the circumstances to make a valid plan for the next day. He slept in a room above the goat stable near the house. A group of soldiers took quarters in an attic above his room.

In his own book "Infantry Attacks" Rommel says, "By the flickering light of the open fire in one of the houses I studied the map thoroughly." There is no mention of the petrol lamp and candles. But this study of the map took place before Rommel has sent Lieutenant Leuze on a reconnaissance mission. It is fair to assume that the briefing in the Brgolič house, as reported by Ivana, is probably the occasion described by Rommel as receiving Leuze's report and forming a plan for the

Above: In the background of this 1936 photo two thatch roofed houses can be seen. Rommel first sought information in the house on the right and was sent to the one on the left, then a village inn, where he met Ivana Šekli. Both houses were destroyed by the 1976 earthquake. Photo: courtesy of Leopold Šekli.

Below: My guides and friends Jožef Stric and Branko Drekonja standing at the site where the house of Ivana Šekli once stood. Photo: author.

Above: a 1914 photo of Ivana Šekli (on the left) who briefed Rommel about the situation in Jevšček. Photo: courtesy of Leopold Šekli.

Below: Mr Leopold Šekli provided valuable information about Rommel's arrival in Jevšček and about Ivana Šekli. Photo: author.

attack on Kraguvenca. It is interesting that Rommel himself doesn't mention Ivana at all. But neither has/did he ever mentioned/mention Antonija Zgaga from Petrovo Brdo. As of/for the Italian prisoner, the locals speak of two deserters who hid in the village. One of them drowned while taking cover in the water tank while the other was captured and interrogated by Rommel and his men. In Rommel's own account the Italian prisoner was brought in by Lieutenant Leuze on his return from his/the reconnaissance patrol.

About his stay in Jevšček, Rommel says, "The exhausted detachment was given another rest period. The bulk of the unit sat within a few yards of the enemy, before the hearthfires in solidly built houses, consuming coffee and dried fruit, which were offered to us by very friendly Slovenes. An occasional shot was heard outside, followed by an Italian hand-grenade burst."

The Brgolič house is now occupied by the grandson of Mrs Marija Šekli (Brgolič), Mr Stane Šekli and his family. Mr Stane Šekli believes that it was his grandmother Marija who prepared food for Rommel himself. He is not quite happy with Rommel's account. According to the family tradition, Marija offered Rommel and his officers not only coffee and dry pears, but proper food as well. This same opinion is echoed by Mr. Leopold Šekli, "This was an area behind the front line with many storehauses. A lot of the provisions stored by the Italian army found their way to the locals as well. That's why the villagers were indeed able to serve the German soldiers real coffee. But they offered them other food as well."

After the First World War, the room above the stable where Rommel spent the night was used by some family members. Between 1945 and 1955, it served as a lodging for Yugoslav border guards until new border control barracks were constructed. In 1982, Mr Stane Šekli extended the old family house and to do that he pulled down the stable and the dwelling above it. "It was hard labour," he remembers. "The little house was very solidly built." Then in 1990, a historian from Ljubljana arrived. Mr Šekli doesn't remember his name, but he recalls the conversation. "What have you done?" apparently the historian said. "What a pity! I've done some study and I'm sure this was the house that Erwin Rommel slept in."

Mr Stane Šekli's father was born in 1913. He was four when the Germans arrived in the village. "My father did mention that during the First World War an important German officer spent the night in that dwelling near the house," recalls Mr Šekli, "but I've never thought twice about it. At least not until the historian told me it was Rommel." There was a good reason why the story about Rommel's stay wasn't passed down to the next generation. The Italians found it very hard to accept that they suffered such a devastating defeat and in 1926 a special military commission investigated the First World War events around Jevšček. The family was afraid that they would be persecuted if the Italians realised they had helped Rommel. So they kept quiet about it. Then, just after the Second World War and with border guards stationed at their property, the fact that during the First World War they had helped the Germans was also better not talked about. Hence Mr Šekli's original ignorance. "Luckily I still have some furniture from that period. I was about to burn the old table, but now that I know it was used during Rommel's conference I'm really glad I didn't." He now plans to re-create Rommel's room in the nearby barn.

Above: an archive photo of the house in which Rommel spent the night. On the right is the main house where he conferred with his officers. In the centre is the adjoining building with the stable below and the stairway leading to the dwelling quarters. Photo: courtesy of Stane Šekli

Below: Mr Stane Šekli and his son Boris in front of their house. While extending it, Mr Šekli demolished the stable where Rommel slept overnight. Photo: author.

Above: Mr Stane Šekli in his lounge room, the same room where, in the evening of October 25, 1917, Rommel conferred with his officers. Photo: author.

Below: the table used during Rommel's briefing in the night of October 25. Photo: author.

Fighting on the Kolovrat ridge, October 25, 1917

A – Disarmament of the advanced post.
B – The breach of the third defence line.
C – Securing of the left flank.
D – Rommel stopped.
E – 2nd Company (Lt. Ludwig) stopped.
F – Rommel attacks.
G – Italians dig in.
H – Machine-gun fire on the Kuk positions.
I – Rommel bypasses Mt Kuk.

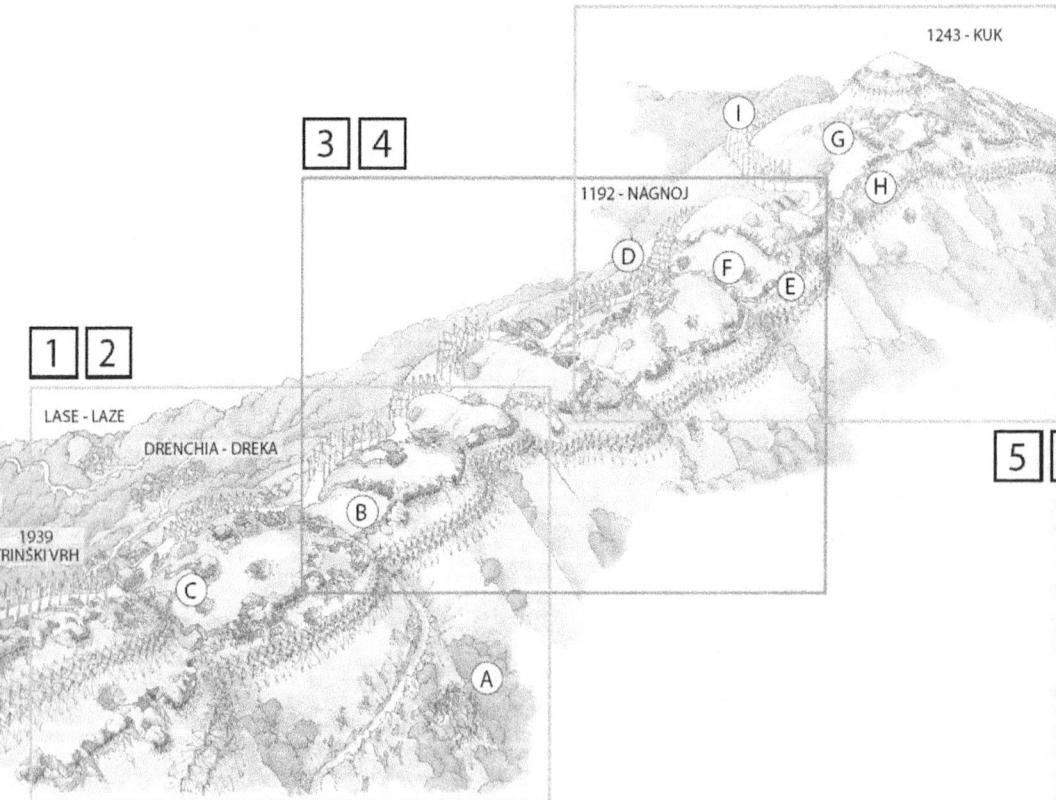

Illustrations on the following three pages depict in detail the breach of the third Italian defence line. Illustrations by the author.

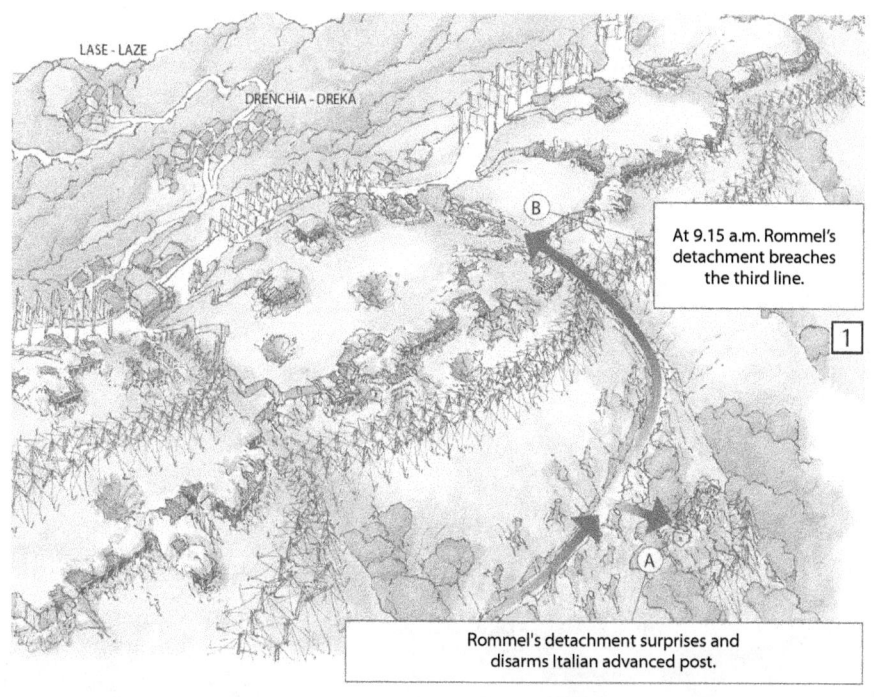

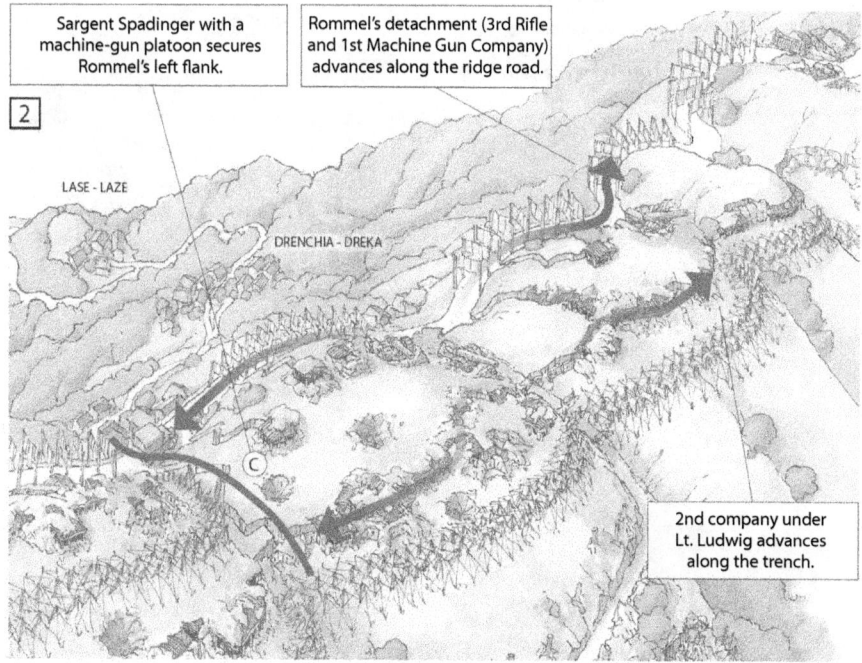

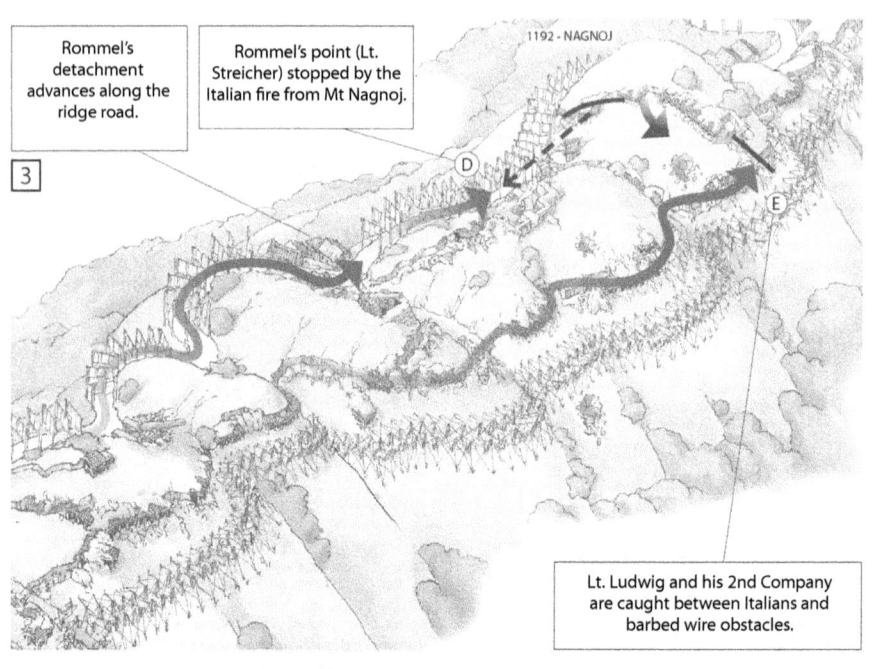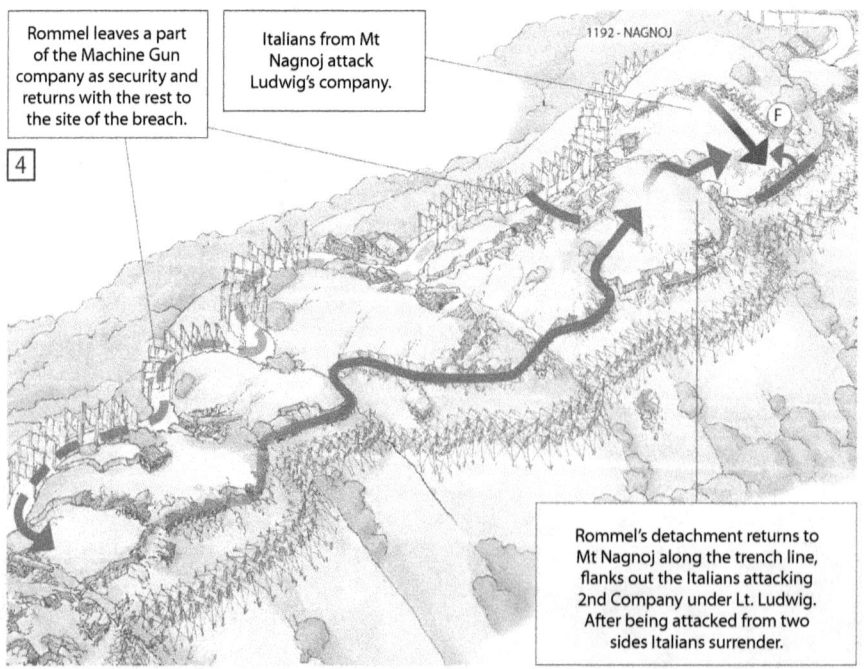

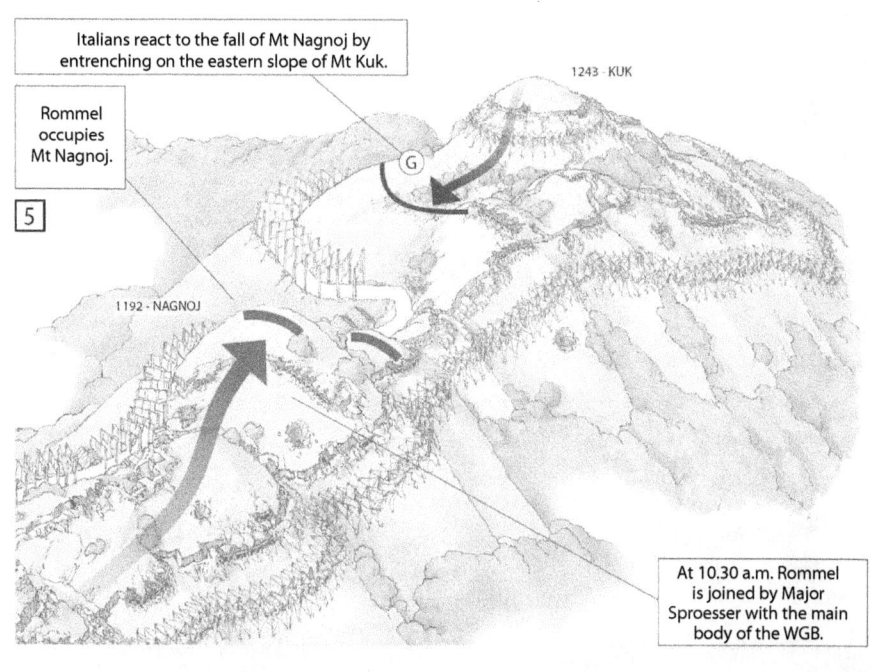

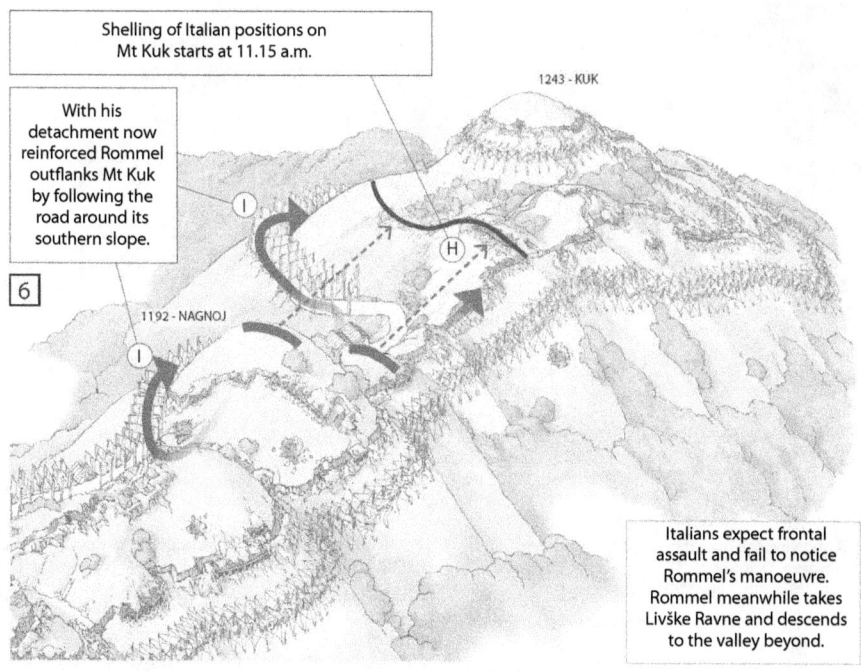

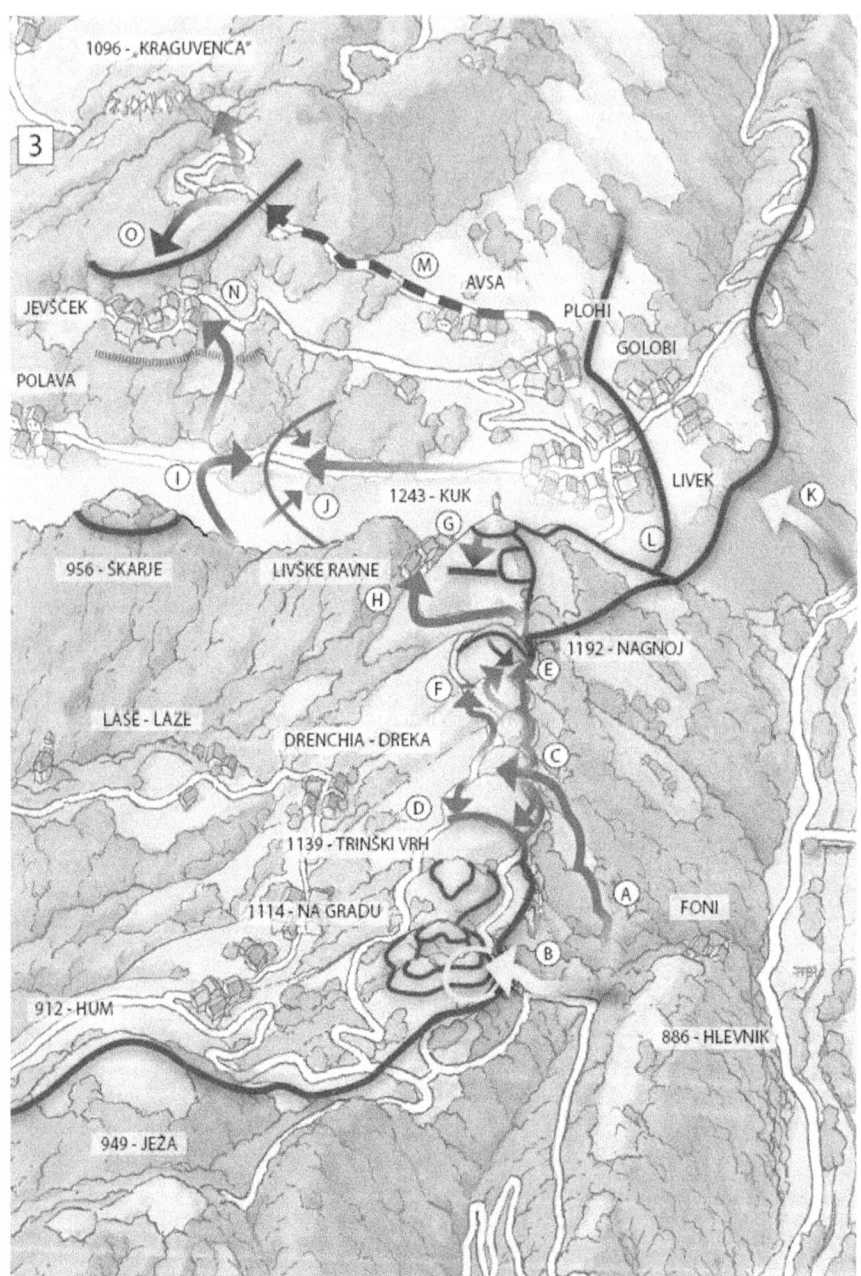

Map 3, showing the operations during the second day of the breach, October 25, 1917 (views from the east and from the south - illustrations by the author).

A – Rommel traverses the northern slope of the Kolovrat ridge.

B – The Leib Regiment attacks the Quote 1114 (na Gradu) but captures only a part of it.

C – Rommel breaches the third Italian line.

D – Sargent Spadinger secures Rommel's left flank.

E – 2nd Company (Lt. Ludwig) is stopped by the Italians.

F – Rommel's detachment stopped. Rommel returns and outflanks the Italians.

G – After the fall of Nagnoj Italians entrench themselves on the slope of Mt Kuk.

H – Rommel's detachment bypasses Mt Kuk and reaches Livške Ravne.

I – Rommel descends into the valley between Mt kuk and Mt Matajur..

J – On the road Livek – Polava Rommel captures the 4th Bersaglieri Brigade.

K – Meanwhile the elements of the 12th Schleswig Division are held back by the Italians.

L – The main body of the WGB attacks Livek from Mt Kuk.

M – With the road to Polava blocked the Italians are retreating towards Mt Matajur.

N – The Italians occupy their reserve positions above Jevšček.

O – Rommel's detachment reaches Jevšček and encamps for the night.

Above: Marija Šekli (Brgolič), seated in the centre, surrounded by her family. Her husband Janez is standing in the background. During WW1 he was an Austro-Hungarian soldier and was wounded on the nearby mountain of Krn. The photo was taken between the two wars, most likely in 1929. Photo: courtesy of Mr Stane Šekli.

Below: Italian entrenched positions above the village of Jevšček. Rommel's unit conquered them on the morning of October 26. Photo: author.

THE THIRD DAY – OCTOBER 26, 1917

During the night Rommel's scouts found a passage around the Italian line above the village and towards the peak of Kraguvenca. The next morning, Rommel left a part of his troops in Jevšček in order to engage the Italians who were occupying the trenches above the village. With the main body of his detachment, he set off uphill. But things did not go according to his plan. The dawn arrived earlier than he anticipated. The Italians on Kraguvenca noticed their approach while they were still quite a long way off and opened fire. Rommel realised that even trying to hold the positions they had reached would be costly. At the same time, the sound of battle behind his back told him that the forces he had left in Jevšček were indeed engaging the Italians above the village, thus preventing them from attacking him from behind.

It was now, in this very difficult position, that Rommel's brilliant military mind demonstrated its full capacity and value. The move he made had nothing to do with the military doctrine of the time and was certainly the very last thing the Italians could have anticipated. He quickly reorganised his unit into some assault teams and descended back towards Jevšček. From the heights above the village his groups attacked the Italians besieging Jevšček from behind. The result was astounding. Not only the particular Italian unit caught between his troops and those in Jevšček, but the entire Italian line, a well-armed regiment with 37 officers and 1600 men, surrendered.

Now the unit left in Jevšček was free to join Rommel's detachment in an attack on Kraguvenca. With Kraguvenca as the main objective and with the element of surprise lost, Rommel saw no option but to charge. In fact, this was his only frontal attack during the entire campaign and his losses were accordingly high. In a couple of moments, both commanders of the 2nd company, First Lieutenant Ludwig and then his replacement, Lieutenant Aldinger, received heavy injuries. But the gain was also big. When he conquered Kraguvenca at 7.15 in the morning, Rommel cut the only escape route for the entire Italian garrisons of Mrzli vrh and Matajur. It seemed as if the operation was finished. But Rommel was not sure. He feared that by securing the gains and allowing his men to have some rest, he could give the Italians a chance to regroup, overrun his positions and escape. So he decided to keep the momentum and continue the pursuit of the enemy.

If I understood Rommel's writing correctly, once the Kraguvenca was taken he had only half a company left at his disposal. He first sent Sergeant Hugel to secure Quote 1192, a rise half way to the peak of Mrzli vrh. From there he was to cover Rommel's advance with machine guns. With the remaining soldiers, he moved up the southwestern slope of Mrzli vrh. On their way, the soldiers kept outflanking individual spots of resistance. Once feeling that they were being bypassed, the Italians would immediately retreat. Seeing that no reinforcements were coming, Rommel kept wondering if he should halt his advance, but each time he was in doubt, he decided against. At 8.30, Hugel's detachment reached Quote 1192. Since he had met with strong resistance, Rommel abandoned his direction of advance and joined Hugel at Quote 1192. He ordered him to pin down the garrison of the Mrzli vrh with machine gun fire while he fetched some reinforcements, hoping that the 12th Division and the WGB were already advancing from Livek up the Matajur road.

During his descent, Rommel bumped into a patrol of Italian 'bersaglieris'. By the time they got their rifles off their shoulders and started firing, Rommel had already disappeared in the bushes. While they chased him downhill, he turned and ascended back to Quote 1192. To avoid getting into a similar situation, he sent a rather strong patrol to Livek.

Above: Stone built Italian positions above Jevšček are still well preserved. Rommel captured them by striking from behind. Photo: author.

Below: Rommel's Mt Kraguvenca (in fact Mt Strmola), as seen from above - from the slope of Mt Mrzli vrh. Photo: author.

The gathering of Rommel's troops was made difficult by countless encounters with small Italian units dotting the battlefield. It was 10 o'clock when Rommel felt strong enough to again continue his advance. First he used rockets to signal the German artillery to shell the Italian position. Then he ordered his machine gunners on Quote 1192 to open covering fire and started his advance along the left side of the ridge, just below the Matajur road, bypassing the Italian positions above them. Noticing the German advance, many Italians started to retreat northwards, towards the right side of the ridge. Rommel didn't bother chasing them but rather advanced further up, towards the peak of Mrzli vrh.

Even during the fight for the Quote 1192 Rommel noticed a large body of soldiers just below the peak of Mrzli vrh. "They were standing about, seemingly irresolute and inactive, and watched our advance as if petrified." he wrote. Had they attacked, thought Rommel, they could have easily fought their way to Kraguvenca. Or they could retreat towards the peak of Matajur. But they just stood idle. Under the peak of Mrzli vrh the Matajur road makes a long turn right, towards the east. Rommel knew that following the road along that long bend would take much longer than cutting the bend through the forest. But his men carrying heavy machine guns were exhausted, so he told them to take the easier trail and follow the road around the bend. He himself, accompanied only by two officers, took the shortcut up through the forest.

When he stepped out of the forest, he faced scores of Italians. Rommel left his two companions waiting in the forest and continued alone. He was approaching the Italians with a handkerchief in his hand. Halfway towards them, he became aware that he had passed the point of no return. If they decided to fire he would have stood no chance. But he kept on approaching. Suddenly the Italians moved. They started to throw their rifles away, ran to Rommel and lifted him onto their shoulders, shouting "Evviva Germania!"

At that moment the remaining detachment of Rommel's came marching firmly around the bend. They started to disarm the Italians. Once realising how few the Germans were, the Italian officers tried to take over the command again. But it was too late. Just under the peak of Mrzli vrh, 1500 men of the First Regiment of the Salerno Brigade were captured.

On interrogating the prisoners, Rommel found out that the Matajur peak was defended by the Second Regiment of the Salerno Brigade, a highly decorated regiment and Rommel assumed its soldiers would put up a stiff resistance. His assumption proved to be justified.

The peak of Mt Mrzli Vrh and the area beneath it, approximately the area of the road bend, where the First Regiment of the Salerno Brigade surrendered to Rommel's detachment. Photo: author.

The way along the ascending ridge from Mrzli vrh towards the peak of Matajur is barred by the rises of Krajec (Quote 1424) and Glava (Quote 1467). The Matajur road bypasses these two rises to the left, along the southern slope. From Krajec and Glava, the Italians controlled the entire western slope of Mrzli vrh. The moment Rommel's men appeared on this side of Mrzli vrh, they were greeted by heavy machine gun fire. Rommel retreated and ordered his machine gunners to take positions for covering fire. He then led his detachment into the gorge below the road and a long way around the southern slope of the Quote 1424. When he was about to attack he received an order that the entire WGB retreat.

He was puzzled as to the reason to do that. Then he concluded that Major Spösser assumed that the 1st Regiment of the Salerno Brigade was an entire Matajur garrison and that the battle was already over. Rommel therefore decided to disregard the order and continue the attack according to his original plan. He and his men climbed uphill, crossed the Matajur road again and surprised the Italians at the southern flank of their positions. The surprised Italians began to retreat from both Krajec and Glava (Quotes 1424 and 1467) towards the northern slope of Matajur. By doing so they exposed themselves to Rommel's machine gunners on Mrzli vrh. When fired upon, they stopped. Rommel and his soldiers climbed on top of a rock so the Italians could see them and started to wave with their handkerchiefs. No-one moved - everything went silent.

Rommel and his group continued along the road. The forest obscured his view for a while, but after a sharp bend an amazing view offered itself to him. 300 metres further the entire Second Regiment of the Salerno Brigade was gathering on the road and laying down its arms. At the edge of the road sat the commander of the Regiment encircled by his officers, weeping with frustration and shame over the insubordination

Above: Mr Jožef Stric and photographer Rafael Marn on the top of Mt Mrzli vrh. The Kanin Massif in the background was also a scene of some heavy WW1 fighting. Photo: author.

Below: The peak of Mt Matajur as seen from Mt Mrzli Vrh. The wooded rise to the left is Krajec (Quote 1424) and the wooded rise to the right is Glava (Quote 1467). Photo: author.

of the soldiers of his once-proud regiment. Rommel was afraid that the Italians might realise how weak his unit really was. So he ordered an immediate separation of the officers from the rest of the prisoners. He directed the 35 officers and 1200 soldiers captured down the Matajur road towards Livek. "The captured colonel fumed with rage when he saw that we were only a handful of German soldiers!" wrote Rommel.

The only remaining task was to neutralise the garrison on the very peak of Mount Matajur. Rommel ordered Lieutenant Leuze to set machine guns for covering fire and started to advance directly towards the peak, going up the ravine in the southern slope. But his detachment was soon stopped by intensive Italian fire. So he returned and instead climbed towards Glava – the Quote 1467. On his way, he kept meeting small groups of Italians converging to the spot where the 2nd Regiment of the Salerno Brigade surrendered. Most of them were already without their weapons. Once on the Quote 1467, Rommel followed the ridge towards the top. On the other side of the ridge, Rommel's soldiers surprised an Italian company firing on some units of the German 12th Division, which were approaching upwards from the north. An attack from behind was the last thing the Italians had expected and they immediately surrendered.

Halfway between Glava (Quote 1467) and the peak of Matajur is a small stony outcrop. Rommel decided to use it as a machinegun stronghold. While they were installing their arms, the garrison at the top gave a sign that they wished to surrender. "One hundred and twenty more men waited patiently until we took them prisoner at the ruined border guardhouse on the summit of Matajur," wrote Rommel.

As they were gathering prisoners at the top of the mountain, Rommel's soldiers were joined by a patrol of six soldiers and one non-commissioned officer of the 23rd Infantry Regiment. As we will see later Rommel felt special need to stress that apart from his unit and the patrol, no-one else was in sight at the top for a very long time. At 11.40 the winners fired four rockets: three green and one white – a sign that the Matajur Massif had been taken. It was safe for the German 12th Division to enter the Nadiža/Natissone gorge just west of Matajur and to roll towards Cividale.

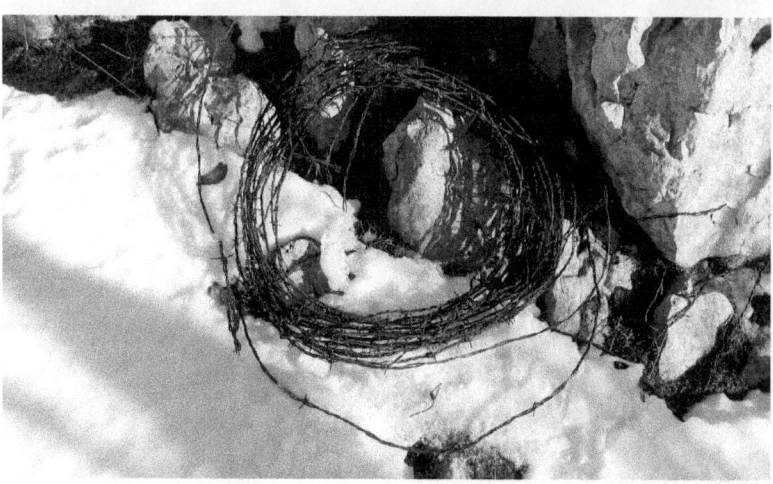

Photographer Rafael Marn posing with the coil of barbed wire found on the top of Mt Mrzli Vrh. Photo: author.

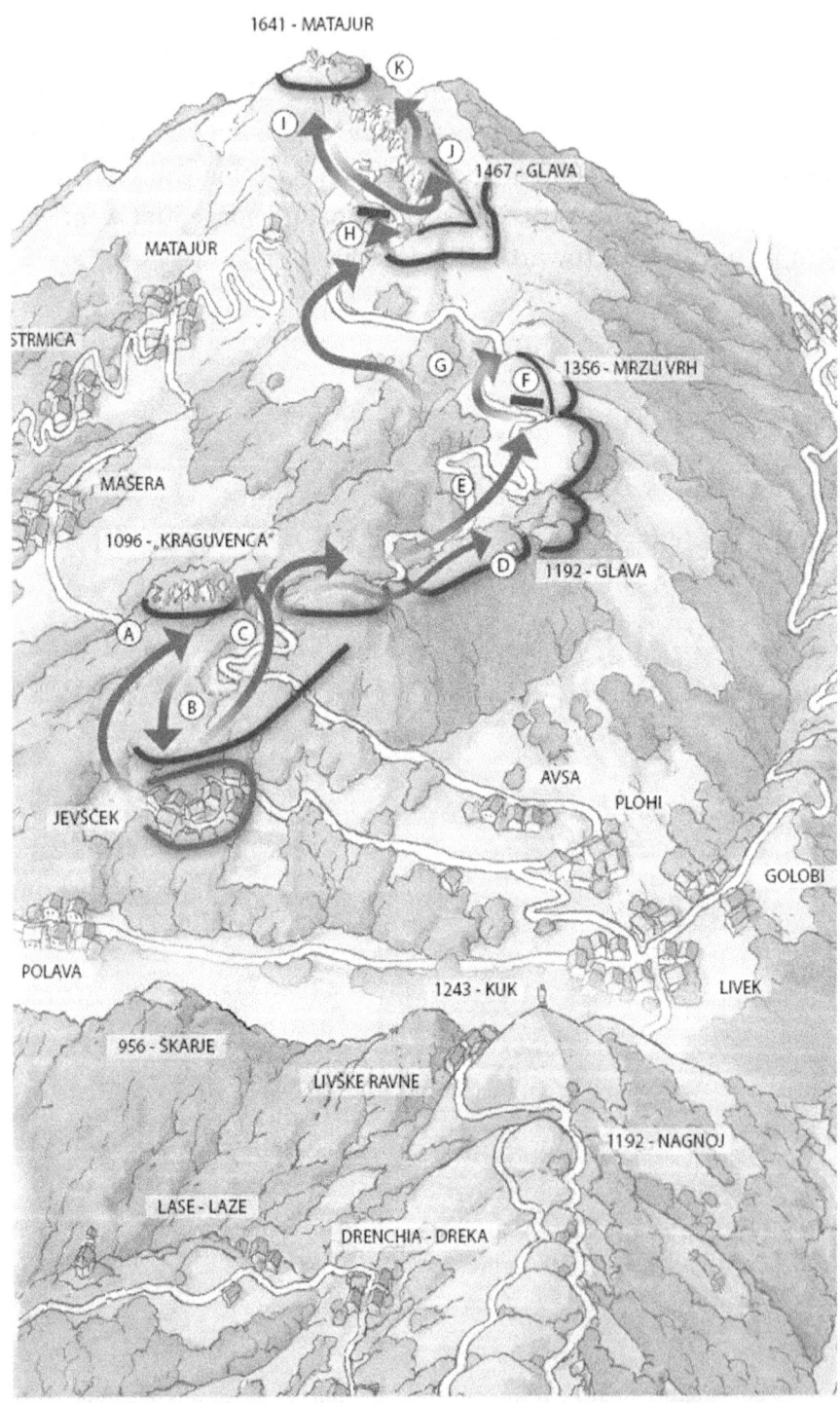

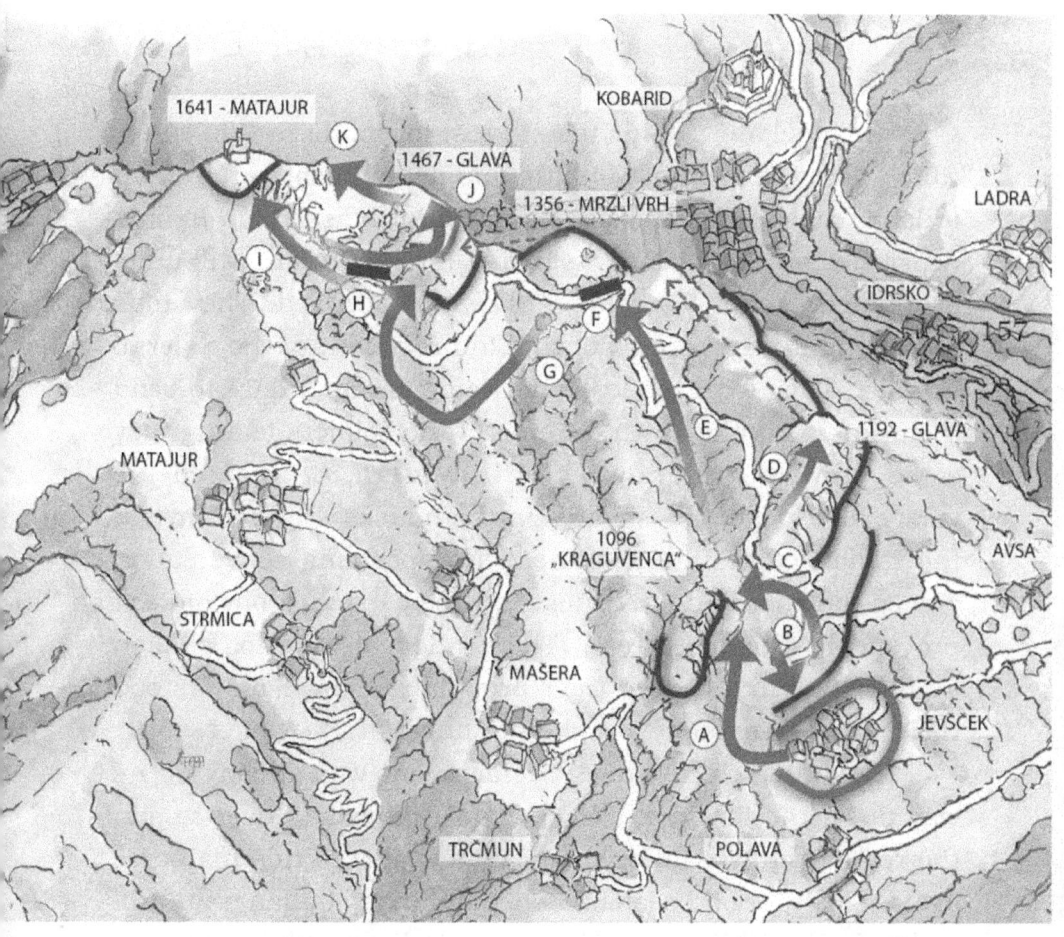

Map 4, showing the operations during the third day of the breach, October 26, 1917 (views from the east and from the south - illustrations by the author).

A – Rommel's morning attempt to surprise the crew of "Mt Kraguvenca" fails.

B - Rommel attacks from above Italian positions above Jevšček. Italians surrender.

C - Reinforced with the crew he left in Jevšček Rommel again attacks "Mt Kraguvenca" and conquers it.

D - Rommel sends Machine Gun platoon under Sgt. Huegel to capture Glava (Quote 1192).

E - Rommel advances towards Mt Mrzli Vrh.

F - Under Mt Mrzli Vrh the 1st Regiment of the Salerno Brigade surrenders to Rommel's detachment.

G - Strong resistance from Glava (Quote 1467) forces Rommel to descend into the gully and to outflank it.

H - Once Rommel's detachment circumvents Glava the 2nd Regiment of the Salerno Brigade surrenders.

I - A frontal attack to the peak of Mt Matajur is repulsed.

J - Rommel's detachment climbs on Glava and turns towards Mt Matajur.

K - Once Rommel's detachment reaches a stony outcrop on the ridge of Mt Matajur the Italians on the top of Mt Matajur surrender.

CHASING THE ENEMY

Rommel allowed his men to rest for an hour. While they were still at the top of Matajur, his detachment received an order to move to the village of Mašera, or Masseris in Italian, which lies on the southern slope of the mountain. Still quite exhausted, Rommel's soldiers slowly descended. They took with them all the officers of the 2nd regiment of the Salerno Brigade. They were restless and Rommel didn't dare to send them into the valley with the rest of the soldiers fearing they could provoke a mutiny. Once in Mašera, he secured the village and lodged his soldiers in the houses. He then invited the Italian officers to a dinner. "No sparkling conversation graced the board and my guests scarcely touched our modest provender," Rommel wrote. "The gentlemen were too shaken by their fate and that of their proud regiment. I understood their plight completely and did not linger at the table."

Before dawn, Rommel's detachment was already on its way down the valley of the Nadiža / Natissone River to join the rest of the WGB. Rommel was now able to ride his horse again. The front had been breached but many Italian units still resisted. The WGB was fighting the Italians at the village of Šentjur or Sanguarzo (Rommel writes San Quarzo), but Major Sprösser left Rommel's detachment out of the fighting that day. The battle stopped at 14.00 in the village of Purgessimo (Prešnje) near Cividale. Meanwhile, Rommel's detachment was enjoying some rest. At midnight, it was sent to Campeglio where it joined the rest of the WGB and then continued in the direction of Ronchis (Ronk) and Faedis (Fojde).

On October 28, German and Austrian forces continued pursuit despite some heavy rain. A group of merry soldiers "found" some umbrellas, but "higher authority soon vetoed this new addition to the table of basic allowance". On the Torre River, near the village of Primulacco, they encountered

Above: This photo of the WGB soldiers resting on the top of the mountain was taken elsewhere. But Rommel's detachment resting on Mt Matajur probably looked very much the same. Courtesy of: Haus der Geschichte Baden-Württemberg.

Below: Once Mt Matajur had been secured the German 12th Division was able to advance along the gorge of the Nadiža / Natissone river towards Cividale. Courtesy of the National Museum of Contemporary History of Slovenia.

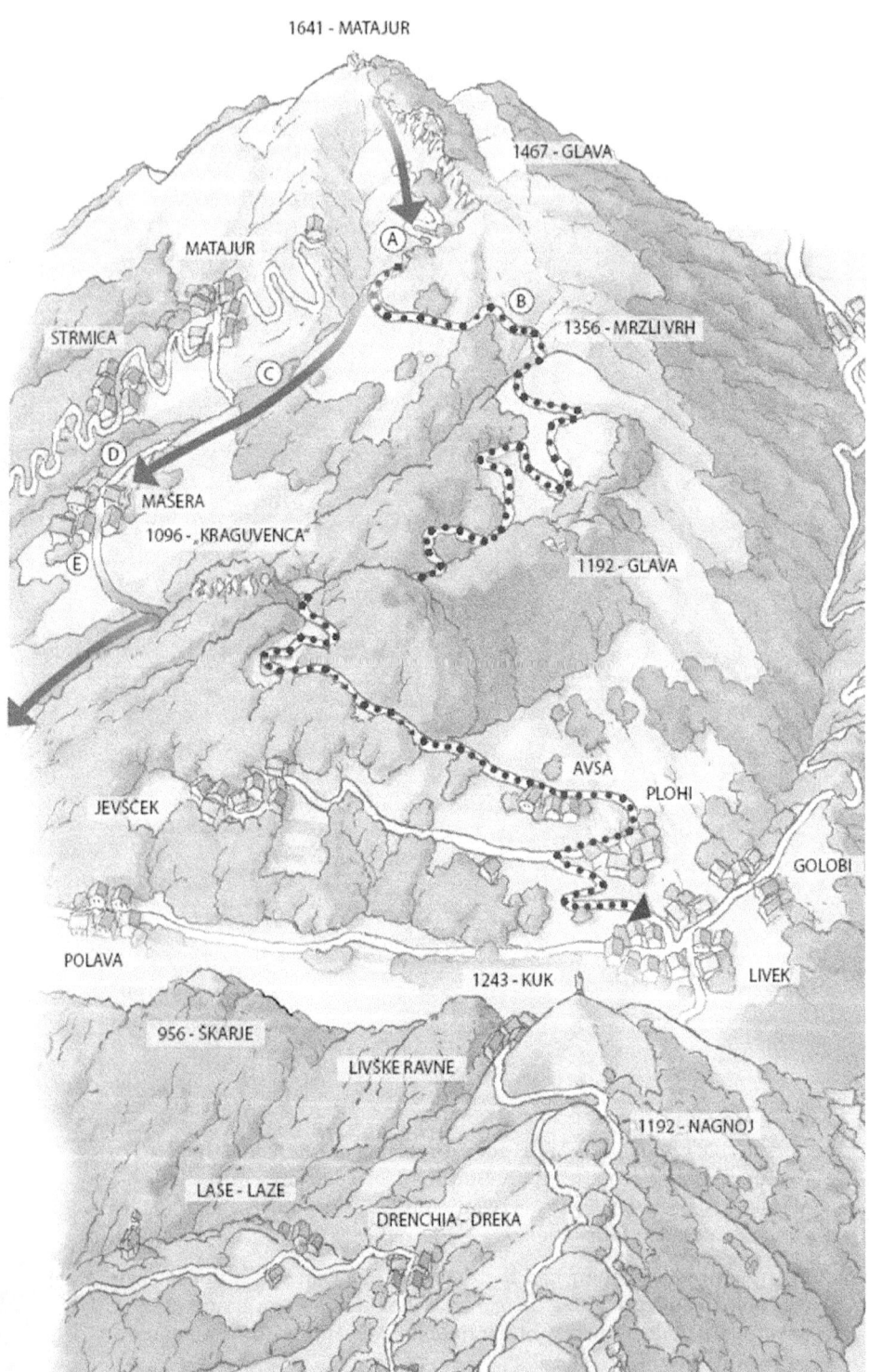

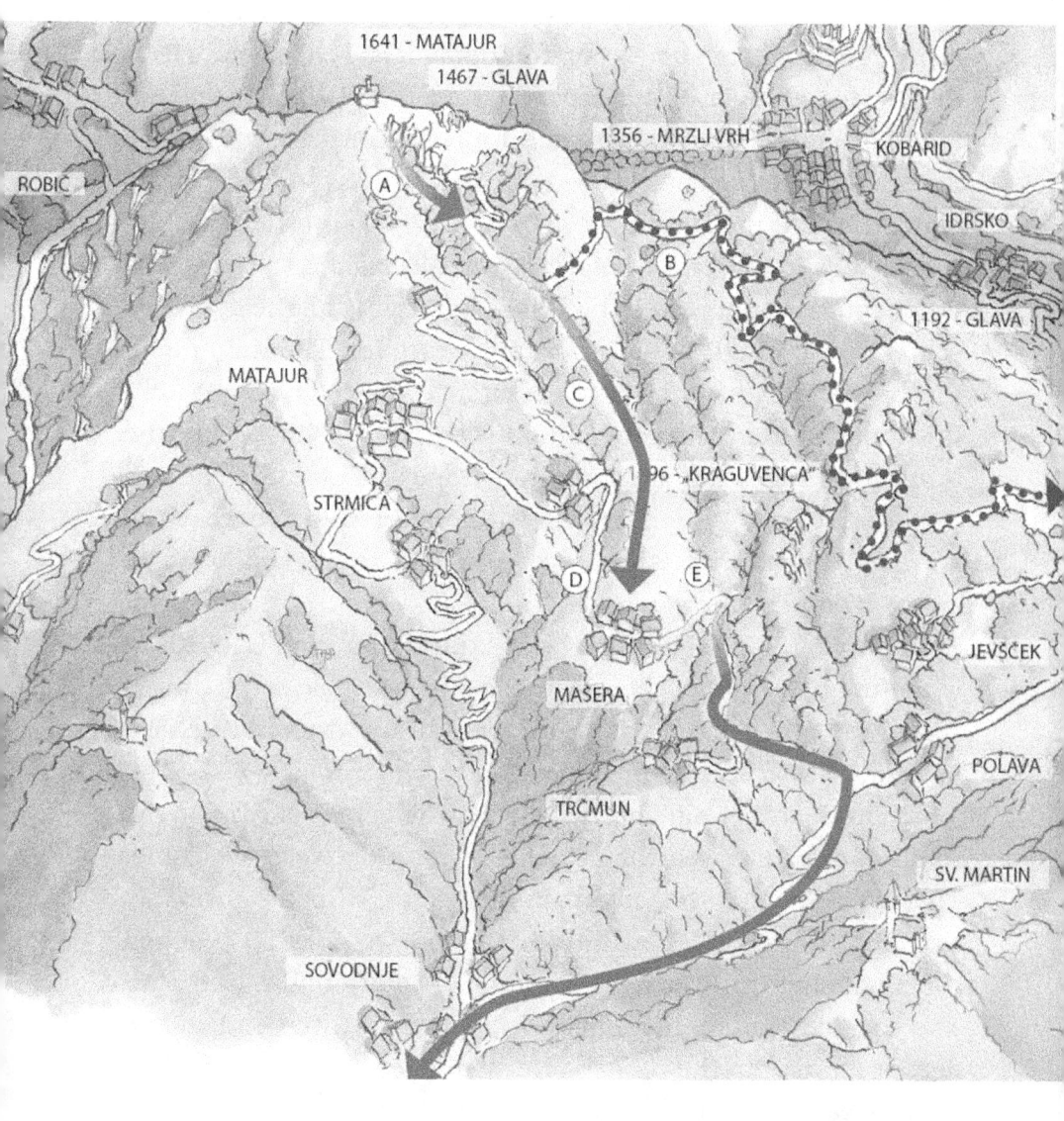

Map 4, showing the operations during the third day of the breach, October 26, 1917 (views from the east and from the south - illustrations by the author).

A – Rommel's detachment returns with the prisoners to the place where the 2nd Regiment of the Salerno Brigade had surrendered.

B - To avoid rebellion Rommel separates captured officers and soldiers. Captured soldiers are sent down the Matajur road.

C - Rommel takes captured officers with him. They descend to the village of Mašera (Masseris).

D - In the village Rommel invites Italian officers to a dinner, but the spirits are low.

E - Rommel stays in the village overnight and the next day catches up with the rest of the WGB which advances towards Cividale.

some Italian resistance from the opposite bank of the river. In the village itself, they discovered an Italian laundry depot and were more than happy to supply themselves with some dry underwear. During the night, they were reinforced by a platoon of the mountain artillery and given an order to build a bridge over the Torre before daybreak. Rommel tried to be practical; he constructed the bridge by driving all the available vehicles that could be found into the stream. The Italians on the opposite bank dispersed after a few artillery shots and the construction went on undisturbed. But at daybreak, the bridge was still unfinished. A strong rope was stretched across the last section of the river and the soldiers waded across the stream. An Italian prisoner carrying a large medical kit was swept away by the current. "I felt sorry for the poor devil. Spurring my horse I galloped after the Italian and succeeded in getting near him in the stream. In his mortal fear the Italian seized the stirrup and the good horse brought us both safely to land," wrote Rommel.

On the other side of the river, in the village of Rizzolo the inhabitants surprised the soldiers with a very warm welcome. The WGA spent the night in "Pagagua" (today probably Fagagna), passed Cisterna and later on October 30 reached the Tagliamento River near Dignano. The orginal Italian plan was to hold the enemy at the Tagliamento River and in the decade leading to the First World War, they constructed a line of forts called "Fortezza Tagliamento". But during the eleven Isonzo Battles, the forts were disarmed and cannons were sent to the front. Still, the advance was actually halted for a couple of days. During this waiting time, Rommel was upset by the news that the German 12th Division had been mentioned as having captured Mount Matajur.

During the night of November 2, the river was finally crossed near the village of Cornino. Rommel gives credit for that to the Reidl Battalion of the 4th Bosnian Regiment. On

Above: Soldiers of German 12th Division approaching Cividale. Courtesy of the National Museum of Contemporary History of Slovenia.

Below: Abandoned Italian military material on the approach to Udine. Italians first planned to put up a resistance on the Tagliamento river, but then retreated all the way to the Piave river. Courtesy of the National Museum of Contemporary History of Slovenia.

November 3, the WGB was detached from the German Alpine Corps and given the mission of breaking through the Carnic Alps as an advance guard of the 22nd Imperial and Royal Division. The plan was to advance along the line Meduno – Claut – Longarone. On November 7, some strong Italian resistance stopped the advance over the Klautana (today Clautana) Pass. Neither flanking manoeuvres nor a night attack brought the desired break-through and Rommel's soldiers returned to the valley. The next day they learned that during the night the Italians had evacuated their positions. Coming over the pass, Rommel was very pleased to see such favourable positions being abandoned without a fight. In Cimolais, a township on the other side of the Clautana pass, an extremely polite Lord Mayor wanted to present Rommel with the key to the Town Hall. But Rommel feared an ambush and had the town secured first. Then the entire WGB had a good meal and a good rest.

Longarone was now very close, but the path there was barred by a defensive line descending from Mount Lodina, closing the valley and ascending to Mount Cornetto. At first sight, the defences seemed unbreachable. But with imaginative maneouvring and inventive combinations of well-harmonised machine gun fire, Rommel managed to force the defenders to retreat. He knew he had to keep up with the enemy and regroup to form an ambush or blow up the bridges. In a narrow valley both could be fatal. So he chased the enemy through San Martino and Erto into the gorge of Vajont, where the road is cut into cliffs and goes through a number of tunnels. Rommel arrived at the Vajont bridge just in time to cut the fuse that was already lit to blow it up. He was able to reach Longarone, the site of his last great victory during this campaign.

Today, Longarone is a name of world renown, but not because of Rommel. For decades his undertaking was overshadowed by another, more macabre event that took

German soldiers partying somewhere in northern Italy after the successful breach of the front on the Soča / Isonzo river. Courtesy of the National Museum of Contemporary History of Slovenia.

place in 1963. Soon after the First World War, in 1920 the idea arose that the gorge of Vajont could be used to build a power plant dam. But it wasn't until 1953 when, despite the opposition of the inhabitants of the area, the electricity company SADE began constructing the dam which was to be "the highest in the World". As soon as the dam was finished and the lake started to fill with the water, the first signs of ground sliding on a rather large scale appeared. Neither SADE nor ENEL, a state owned company that took over the project in March1963 seemed to be alarmed by these signs. Apparently the geologists claimed that the sliding would happen slowly, in a controlled manner.

So all the warning signs were neglected until on October 9, 1963 at 10.30 pm about 260 million cubic metres of soil, rocks and trees slid at a great speed into the lake. Displaced water formed a wave that, upon hitting the dam, climbed 250 metres high above the dam and then crashed to the township below. The exact number of victims has never been determined. It is assumed that between 1,900 and 2,500 of the inhabitants of Longarone and other villages down the Piave river valley perished. Today, the city centre is notably different from other settlements in the area. It looks very modern since not a single building within the centre itself predates the year 1963. The dam, on the other hand, still stands intact – a splendid piece of engineering. In 2008, it became a monument of the tragedy which UNESCO included on a list of five great disasters to warn mankind of the consequences of careless interference with the natural environment. Both villages that Rommel passed through in November 1917, San Martino and Erto, are ghost towns now – just like the dam, they are monuments to failed human endeavours.

Part 3
HONOUR AND GLORY

A QUESTION OF HONOUR

On 26 August 1278, on the Marchfeld, near the village of Dürnkrut, which the Czechs call Suché Kruty, two armies clashed in a battle that was to determine the fate of Central Europe for centuries to come. In fact, the result of that battle still echoes in the present ethnic makeup of this part of the continent. The army of Emperor Rudolf I of Habsburg defeated the army of the Czech King, Otokar II Přemysl. The Czech King lost his life. The lands that he had conquered in the previous two decades - Upper and Lower Austria, Styria, Carinthia, Carniola and Friul - now, one after another, passed into the personal, hereditary ownership of the Habsburg family. With this the "poor Swiss Count" acquired what was to be the basis for what history describes as the Habsburg Empire.

There is an interesting detail that not a single historian omits to mention when speaking about this battle: it was not conducted in accordance with the rules of engagement of the day. The battle was decided by the intervention of troops who were previously hidden behind the nearby rises and the woods and unexpectedly attacked Otokar's troops from the flank. This sort of conduct was then regarded as dishonourable and reportedly Rudolf's commander, Ulrich von Kapellen, apologised beforehand to his men for having to lead them in such a charge.

Yet it was with the very same kind of maneouvres that

Erwin Rommel achieved his successes. He searched the opponent's weak spots, bypassed the enemy and attacked his flank or rear. Did he ever wonder just how honourable his conduct was? If so, what was his opinion? He may have thought that this was an issue for contemporaries while history judges warlords mostly on merit, on the degree to which the achieved result justifies the means that were utilised.

It is probably fair to assume that he simply wasn't bothered with questions of this sort. By the onset of the First World War, the times of medieval chivalry had irrevocably passed or, worse, they had turned, in a rather perverse manner, into the very opposite. How else to explain that stiff aristocratic Italian officers did not measure their successes by territorial gains but rather by the number of their fallen soldiers. Rommel strived for the opposite: he tried to achieve as much as possible with as few losses as possible. This probably was not just because military logic would suggest saving human "material", but out of sincere consideration for his men. Describing the approach to Kraguvenca, for example, he wrote, "At this moment the responsibility for the lives of my officers and men weighed very, very heavily on me; I had to extricate them from the danger of which they were oblivious."

The issue in Rommel's breaches therefore was not that of honour, but of doctrine. The reason that the opponent failed to predict his moves was not that they were dishonourable, but rather that they differed quite notably from the prevailing doctrine of the time. Accepted doctrine demanded that the opponent be attacked frontally. First an artillery barrage was to 'soften up' the enemy by destroying the enemy's positions and wire obstacles and create a passage through them which the infantry unit would then use to approach. Accepted doctrine then prescribed the conquest of positions with the massive onslaught of the "human wave". With cool mathematical precision it calculated in advance the losses and marked them as "acceptable". Rommel avoided these "acceptable" losses by not attacking frontally as the doctrine commanded. Rather than taking his men in front of the barrels, as the enemy was expecting, he led them around and attacked from a direction that no-one was expecting. He attacked in a way that the then prevailing doctrine had no answer for.

INFILTRATION TACTICS

In his Divine Comedy, Dante Alighieri describes how he encounters characters in hell whose only sin was inactivity. Even in antiquity, it was necessary for the survival of the community that every able-bodied member took up arms and participated in defence. It was also necessary to persist in a tight formation in the times when such a formation was the most efficient mode of fighting, the formation being either a Greek phalanx or an infantry unit which, even as late as in the nineteenth century, had to form a square to fend off a cavalry attack. In such times, the courage and perseverance of each individual ensured the solidity of the formation while the escape of one man could bring about its disintegration. To persist in fighting in tight formation and to look the enemy bravely in the eye became a matter of honour if a given community was to survive in the case of being attacked. But to advance in tight formation against a machine gun was no longer a question of honour, but of a clear mind. So the question of honour started to move elsewhere. How honourable was an order given by the officers to their subordinates to charge frontally on machine gun nests through rows of barbed wire obstacles while even in the first, but especially in the second, third and the fourth year of the First World War it became perfectly obvious that such charges could only result in the carnage of the attackers.

This was very well illustrated in the grand 1981 Australian movie "Gallipoli" depicting a futile attack on the hill Nek. High staff officers who demanded their subordinate officers who, in turn, demanded their soldiers to gallantly face death, hardly had any moral justification. Yet they gave such orders over and over again.

At least during the American Civil War, in the battle of Fredericksburg on December 13, 1862, it become painfully clear that the strength and precision of modern armaments no longer justifies an advancement of units, marching straight forward in tight formations, proudly upright. In the most famous episode of the battle, about 3000 defending Confederate soldiers took cover behind a stone wall along a road crossing the battlefield. In 14 charges on the wall, the Northern Army lost between 6000 and 8000 men. One of the Northern officers, Colonel Nelson Miles suggested to his immediate superior, General John Caldwell, abandoning the tactic of approaching in tight formation and rather try by running towards the enemy. Caldwell coldly declined his proposal – the sense of duty and honour were stronger than reason. It was Colonel Miles who paid with his life for Caldwell's sense of honour. Caldwell himself was wounded in this battle. Military strategists also learnt little from trench warfare during the siege of Petersburg.

But unfortunate Colonel Miles wasn't the only one thinking of alternatives. British military instructor Major McMahon published his views in 1909. He suggested abandoning the initial artillery shelling that announced to the enemy the arrival of a massive infantry attack, the so called "human wave". Instead, he proposed the fast moving of small units, supported by a simultaneous covering fire by machine guns and artillery. The aim of these units would be "infiltration", the breach of the front line by concentrating on a single weak spot, followed by penetration into the enemy's back or flank. But the British began to use this tactic only in the third year of the First World War, in February 1917.

On the basis of his own experience, French Captain Andre Laffargue published a pamphlet in 1915 entitled, "A study of attack in the current period of the war". His basic thesis was that the first wave of attack identifies the strongest centres of resistance, but avoids them and advances past them, leaving their destruction to the next wave. French military leaders were not interested in the booklet, nor were their British colleagues. But the Germans supposedly translated it as soon as they got hold of some copies in 1916 and supplied it to their units, regardless of the fact that by then they had already developed their own infiltration tactics.

On the eastern front, the first to utilise infiltration tactics on a massive scale was General Alexei Brusilov, simply called "He" in awe by both his own soldiers and by the enemy. The success of his offensive lasting from June to September 1916 was attributed to small, specially trained units attacking the weakest spots of the enemy's defence and opening passages for the rest of the army. Apparently only Brusilov's successes convinced the French and Germans of the merit of this tactic over the "human wave". Both started to form special units that same year while the British, as mentioned, followed suit only the next year.

But the most famous units, formed to utilise infiltration tactics were German "sturmtruppen", called also "stosstruppen". The origin of these units can be traced to March 1915 when a special unit was formed within the German 8th Army, called "Sturmabteilung Calsow" after the commander, Major Calsow. It is interesting to note that among the unit's equipment were body armour and shields. Despite Calsow's protests the command used his unit mainly as a fast reinforcement of especially endangered sectors. The result was a high casualty rate and ultimately Caslow's replacement. His successor, Captain Willy Rohr summed up general experiences from the front and previous experiences of the unit and introduced some changes in the organisation of the unit and in tactics. The basic battle formation became a squad (a platoon) and standard cannons were replaced by a lighter and more movable model. Apart from the helmet, which later became famous as the German helmet M16, body armour was abandoned, long infantry rifles were replaced by shorter carbines, importance was given to automatic weapons and flame throwers were added to the armament. To facilitate a stealth approach to enemy lines patches on the knees and elbows were added to uniforms, but the real trademark of these units became the linen bags for carrying hand grenades.

The new unit was first tested in 1915 in the Vosges. Encouraged by the result some hunters' battalions were trained in the same manner. The commander of the 8th Army, General Oskar von Hutier was enthusiastic about the effects of the infiltration tactics. He summed it up in four points:

1. Short, but intensive artillery barrage with interchanging explosive and gas shells. The aim of this shelling is not to destroy, but to incapacitate the enemy's defence line.

2. In the cover of artillery barrage, assault units move forward in a spread out formation, avoiding, if possible, a direct conflict, break through the defences on the previously established weak spot and attack the opponent's headquarters and artillery positions.

3. Assault units are followed by infantry battalions armed with light automatic weapons and flame throwers, attacking along narrow sectors and destroying strong resistance positions circumvented by the assault teams. The actions of these units are supported by mine throwers and light artillery capable of following the advance and enhancing it when necessary.

4. In the last phase, a regular infantry attacks and neutralises the remaining enemy's forces still offering some resistance.

In September 1917, the Germans successfully used these tactics during the siege of Riga. But as the most successful application of the infiltration tactics in that same year is considered the October breach of the front at Kobarid or, as we read in the book "Infantry Attacks", the breach at Tolmin. I guess there is no need to repeat the name of the man who translated the described tactics from theory into praxis with such amazing success.

In the year 1918, the use of special assault units trained to carry out infiltration tactics became not only acceptable, but necessary. Both on the Allied and on the German side "Sturmtruppen" were now a crucial warfare element, which became most evident during the operation "Michael", the great German offensive against the Western Allies in March 1918.

Much craved for *Pour Le Merite*, also known as the *Blue Max* or *Blauer Max* in German. Photo of a replica: author.

THE QUESTION OF HONOUR
– THE SECOND TIME

The country I live in now is quite different from the one in which I grew up. In that country and in those days all the students who enrolled to study at university were able to postpone their mandatory military service until the end of their studies. But instead they had to undergo two weeks of intense military training. So it happened that hundreds of my fellow students and I found ourselves at a military training camp on a plateau southwest of Ljubljana. We executed manoeuvres called "a squad in advance" and "a squad in defence". We all laughed, asking ourselves, "Is this a First World War re-enactment or what?" After the artillery barrage, symbolised by the explosion of a smoke can, we rushed from an imaginary trench and through an imaginary opening in the barbed wire and formed a skirmish line to advance towards the imaginary adversary. While drilling the defensive action, we would cease fire at the command and retreat to a reserve line. From there we would again attack the imaginary adversary who had no time to consolidate in our first line and was therefore successfully pushed out of our positions. We thought the whole thing funny since we all knew from movies and documentaries that modern warfare is no longer conducted this way. The tactics of infiltration introduced at such a painstakingly slow pace during the First World War has become the prevailing mode of infantry warfare.

But during the First World War, this doctrine was by no means taken for granted. Most officers commanding in the First World War were trained in different times and fought in different wars. They were brought up in the spirit of values such as courage and honour. But we shall now take a step backwards and look at the question of honour from a different side. We shall no longer consider honour as an inner feeling about which conduct on a battlefield is the correct one and which dishonourable, but rather inspect the meaning of the word honour as a way of awarding someone for his achievements. In the light of what was then considered "honourable conduct" and the described slow and gradual introduction of infiltration tactics, we can understand the squabbles about the very desirable award *Pour le Merite* and the seemingly incredible "mistake" that saw recognition for the conquest of Kolovrat and Matajur being awarded to men who were not even there at the time.

True, when it comes to the conquest of the Quote 1114 Na Gradu, the ambitions and vanity of the commander of the Leib Regiment, Major Bothmer, may have played a role. The fact that he had forbidden Rommel to continue his activities strongly implies such a motive. But from this point onward we can assume that the judgment of the command of the Alpine Corps was not led simply by sheer ambition and vanity. We can easily assume that they considered it unthinkable not to award Lieutenants Ferdinand Schörner and Walter Schnieber. The two officers had bravely faced the enemy while charging frontally, as prescribed by the old doctrine – as opposed to this fellow Rommel who kept avoiding enemy fire. Instead of 'braving death' he kept circumventing hostile positions and as a rule he forced the enemy to surrender without a fight by surprising him from behind. Besides, he usually even achieved all this without suffering any casualties of his own. What did the old-time officers think of this mode of conducting warfare? Did they consider it wise? Or did they regard it as underhand and deceitful rather than honourable and therefore unworthy of an officer - especially if such an officer was also an aristocrat, which indeed many of the German officers of the time were.

As we know now, on October 25 Lieutenant Ferdinand Schörner, an officer of the Bavarian Leib Regiment, bravely but without the desired effect attacked the Quote 1114 Na

Gradu. Meanwhile, Rommel moved stealthily below the Italian trench line on Kolovrat, searching for a weak spot that would enable him to breach the defences. Once he broke through, he moved sideways – along the enemy's own trenches and from behind – along the Italian mountain road to destroy the garrison on the ridge. He neutralised the Italians who were attacking with superior forces from the top of Nagnoj by an unexpected attack into the flank. Then he completely avoided any contact with the enemy by descending into the valley of Livek. There he laid an ambush and in that way captured the entire 4th Bersaglieri Brigade. Meanwhile the garrison of the Quote 1114 Na Gradu surrendered because it was cut off rather than conquered. Rommel's actions were in perfect accordance with the principles of General Oskar von Hutier, but these principles were not yet universally accepted. The decision of Major Bothmer to declare as a conqueror of Quote 1114 Na Gradu his own subordinate, Lieutenant Schörner, may not have simply been an expression of vanity, but also an expression of the doctrine of the time and its values. We could speculate that Major Bothmer sincerely believed that someone sneaking around dodging enemy fire could not possibly be regarded as a hero, but only someone bravely confronting the enemy eye-to-eye.

The same situation applies for the conquest of Matajur. The units of the German 12th Division were climbing up its northern slopes, attacking frontally the entrenched Italian positions, but it was conquered by a single WGB company that attacked from an unexpected direction and cut off beforehand the defenders' connection with the rest of their army. The case of an Italian company captured by surprise just below the peak of the mountain while the Italians were fending off the German advance upwards on the northern slope is also very illustrative. There was no doubt whatsoever that all the Italian units, both the regiments of the Salerno Brigade and the 120 defenders of the very peak of Matajur, were captured by Rommel's detachment. Yet in the end the victory was attributed to Lieutenant Walter Schnieber who had at that time reached only the Quote 1325, a rise three hundred metres below the peak of Matajur. Was that really a mistake? I prefer to believe that the same logic as described above was at work and that the command of the 12th Division would not have the honour removed from one of its own people just because of a man who was 'sneaking around'. They preferred to award someone that was not only one of their own, but who had also bravely faced the enemy in accordance with the old doctrine of honour, even if he actually failed to fulfil the task for which the German commander Otto von Below had personally promised the craved for *Pour le Merite*.

Rommel had a good reason to be offended. In his writing he stressed both the fact that, apart from being joined by a small patrol, no-one else came to the peak of Matajur and that the 12th Division was able to advance over Livek and down the Nadiža (Natissone) valley only after the Italian garrisons on Kraguvenca, Mrzli Vrh and Matajur had been captured. But he had to wait for the deserved recognition.

On Kraguvenca, he had to order a frontal attack. The same thing happened at the town of Cimolais. Well-organised defensive positions left Rommel no other choice but to charge directly towards the enemy. But even at Cimolais his exceptional planning, his correct prediction of the psychological effects of his manoeuvres and the good training of his troops capable of carrying out his plans awarded him a victory without a single life lost on his side.

He then continued a hot pursuit of the enemy down the gorge of Vajont and established a blockade of the Piave river valley that entrapped the retreating Italian forces. At least in these last actions there seemingly was not anything that would discredit the prevailing doctrine. At Lavarone his brave stand against the numerically vastly superior enemy was certainly a typical image of heroism. Was it because of that that he was finally allowed to receive his *Pour le Merite*? Or was it that his superiors had realised that an injustice had been done to him at Kolovrat and Matajur and hurried to mend it?

Whatever the case, it was Erwin Rommel who had on the ridges of Kolovrat and Matajur proved the value of infiltration tactics and demonstrated how important it is to maintain an initiative even after the primary tactical goal has been achieved. These were elements which, during the Second World War, thanks to the use of armoured vehicles and aircraft, the Germans successfully transplanted from the tactical to the strategic level in the form of the so-called 'Blitzkrieg'. During the invasion of Poland, Rommel observed the direction in which the development was moving. After the Polish campaign, he secured himself a command of an armoured division. Into the functioning of this division, he introduced the same elements that had already brought him successes on Kolovrat and Matajur, but this time round on a much bigger scale. If not in France then in Africa, these elements earned Rommel world acclaim. He became famous.

Glory was something Rommel wasn't shying from. Even though the expression 'media star' was not yet in use in those days, he was definitely a celebrity and he clearly relished the role. We may try to guess to what degree his vanity was also a moving force behind his actions. Yet no-one has ever denied his commanding abilities and his military achievements. But in addition to all of this, he had another characteristic that secured him his place in the world's history: his persistence on primary moral standards. In the end, this may have brought him a death sentence, but besides the glory, it secured him respect. Respect from everybody, allies and enemies alike.

CONCLUSION

Near Tolmin, at the congruence of the Tolminka and the Soča rivers a strange stone construction stands. From a distance, it may seem to an observer to be a suburban terrace house left in a forest by mistake. There is a building with a long, fenced off garden adjoining it. But once the observer comes closer, it becomes clear that the object is much too serious and too monumental to be anybody's abode. There is another curious detail. The stone used to build the structure is a stark contrast to the bright local limestone. It is dark, heavy granite. It was brought here from the distant Bavarian Alps; for this is the last resting place of 965 German soldiers, fallen during the Kobarid breach.

There is no doubt in my mind that was it not for Erwin Rommel, both the ossuary and the adjoining cemetery would have been much larger. Whether or not the breach would have succeeded without Rommel is a speculation, but that his highly efficient actions have saved a great many lives seems obvious.

Again let us remember the little detail from the beginning: in the wake of the 12th Isonzo Battle the Commander of the German Alpine Corps, General Otto von Bellow personally promised the *Pour le Merite* award to the first German officer who reached the peak of Mount Matajur. So what did Erwin Rommel do to deserve his *Pour le Merite*? He breached two enemy lines, captured the garrisons holding three strategically important mountain peaks, probably saved thousands of lives and ushered in a new military doctrine.

Besides, he was the first German officer to reach the peak of Mount Matajur.

Sources

Douglas – Home, Charles: *Rommel*; translation: Bogdan Gradišnik; Borec, Delo, Ljubljana, 1976.

Galić, Lovro; Marušič, Branko: *Tolminsko mostišče* I and II, Tolminski muzej, Tolmin, 2005.

Group of Authors: *Atlas Slovenije*, Mladinska knjiga and Geodetski zavod Slovenije, Ljubljana, 1985.

Group of Authors: *History of the Second World War*, Macdonald & Co (Publishers) Ltd, 1989.

Group of Authors: *Stoletje svetovnih vojn*, Cankarjeva založba, Ljubljana, 1981.

Instituto Idrografico della Marina: *Carte stradali delle regioni 1:250.000 – Veneto*, Studio F.M.B. Bologna.

Irwin, David: *Rommel*, translation: Stanko Jarc, DZS, Ljubljana, 1980, (izvirnik: The Trail of the Fox, Hoffman und Campe Verlag, Hamburg 1978).

Kaufmann, Joe E.; Kaufmann, Wanda; Jankovič Potočnik, Aleksander; Tonić Vladimir: *The Atlantic Wall - History and Guide*, Pen & Sword, Barnsley, 2012.

Von Lichem, Heinz, *Der Einsame Krieg, Erste Gesamtdokumentation des Gebirgkriegs 1915-1918 von den Julischen Alpen bis zum Joch*; Verlagsanstalt Athesia - Bozen (Bolzano), 1981 (7th edition, 1999).

Ortner, Christian: *Sturmtruppen: Österreichisch-ungarische Sturmformationen und Jagdkommandos im Ersten Weltkrieg*; Verlag Militaria, Wien, 2005.

Rommel, Erwin: *Infanterie greift an*; Feldpostausgabe, Ludwig Voggenreiter Verlag, Potsdam, 1942.

Rommel, Erwin: *Infantry Attacks*; Zenith Press, Minneapolis, USA, 2009.

Rommel, Erwin: *Infantry Attacks*; Frontline Books, Pen & Sword Books Limited, Barnsley, England, 2012.

Rommel, Erwin: *Preboj pri Tolminu*, translation: Miloš Šulin, Kobariški muzej, Kobarid, 1997.

Sapač, Igor: *Grajske stavbe v zahodni Sloveniji, knjiga 4, Brda in Zgornje Posočje*, Viharnik, Ljubljana, 2011.

Štepec, Marko: *Vojne fotografije 1914–1918*, Defensor and Muzej novejše zgodovine Slovenije, Ljubljana, 2008.

Wikipedia, internet encyclopedia.

Archive Material

Bundesarchiv (Wikipedia, Creative Commons): 28, 38
Drekonja Branko: 63
Haus der Geschichte Baden-Württemberg: 3, 16, 19, 22,
    23, 103
Imperial War Museum (Wikipedia, public domain): 31
Joe E. Kaufmann: 34
Muzej novejše zgodovine Slovenije (National Museum of Contemporary History of Slovenia):
    47, 48, 54, 62, 64, 65, 83, 103, 107, 109
Pirih Florjan: 63
Zgaga Rudolf: 51, 52, 53

Photographs

All contemporary photos were taken by the author, except:
Rafael Marn: 51, 52

Illustrations and Maps

Aleksander J. Potočnik: 44, 56, 57, 60, 61, 67, 72, 73, 84, 85, 86,
    87, 88, 89, 100, 101, 104, 105

About the Author

Apart from being the leading Slovenian fortification expert Aleksander Janković Potočnik is also an illustrator and writer. He graduated in 1984 at the Faculty of Architecture at the University of Ljubljana. Despite his formal education as an architect his main endeavour was illustrating and cartooning for the then major Slovenian periodicals. Between 1989 and 1994 he was living in Melbourne, Australia, where he completed a Graduate Diploma course in Animation and Interactive Multimedia. He spent the nineties working mostly as an illustrator and for the advertising industry. In the year 2000 he contributed the animation for the Golden Drumstick Award winning web site at the Golden Drum Festival. Notable was also his animated advertisement for the German based Bayer-Pharma. One of his favourite activities was also drawing pictorial maps.

The turning point in his career happened in October 1999, when drawing a tourist map of the municipality of Žiri. While doing so he came across the remnants of the fortified line that were until then completely unknown to the general public. Under the mentorship of the American fortification expert, Joe E. Kaufmann, he undertook some research and published the very first study about the Rupnik Line in the British based Fort Magazine in 2001. Since then he has published many articles and several books about the subject. The books printed in English or in a bilingual version include:

The Ring of Wire (Utrjena Ljubljana), Ad Pirum, 2006

Slovenian Fortifications (Utrdbe na Slovenskem), Ad Pirum, 2008

Fortifying Europe's Soft Underbelly, Merriam Press, 2012

Hemingway's Trail of the Novel A Farewell to Arms, Merriam Press, 2013

He contributed illustrations for books by Joe E. Kaufmann: The Maginot Line - History and Guide and The Atlantic Wall – History and Guide, both published by British based publishers Pen & Sword.

Aleksander J. Potočnik is a member of the Ad Pirum Institute and also works part time for the Institute for the Protection of Cultural Heritage of Slovenia. He is a member of the Fortress Study group (FSG) and of the Hemingway Society. In the period 2011 – 2013 he was a vice-president of the Association of the Slovenian Fine Artists Societies. At present he is a member of the Art Council of the Fine Art Society of Ljubljana.

ACKNOWLEDGEMENTS

This book was made possible by the resolution of Ad Pirum Institute's director Anton Marn to record the stories of some well-known individuals who were in one way or another related to the fighting in the Soča – Isonzo valley during the First World War. His brother Rafael Marn contributed some superb photography for the glossy Slovenian edition of this book.

My special thanks for helpful advice go to Mr Željko Cimprič and Jože Šerbec. I would also like to thank Ms Damjana Fortunat Černilogar of the Tolmin Museum and Ms Katja Mrakič of Strgulc House in Bovec.

Dr Stephan Kirchberger of the Haus der Geschichte Baden-Württemberg as well as Mr Marko Štepec and Ivo Vraničar of the National Museum of Contemporary History of Slovenia contributed invaluable archive photographic material.

Some advice and material was also contributed by Mr Uroš Košir, Mr Branko Drekonja, Mr Florjan Pirih, Mr Joe E. Kaufmann, Mr Leopold Šekli and Mr Rudolf Zgaga. I'm also grateful to Mr Leopold Šekli and to Mr Rudolf Zgaga for their testimonies. Mr Jožef Stric kindly guided me to some particular locations on Kolovrat Ridge and Mt Matajur where the events of October 1917 took place.

The staff of the Bežigrad Library and of the National and University Library in Ljubljana were most helpful when looking for bibliographical material.

Finally I would like to thank Mr Anton Marn for his advice and help in composing this book and Ms Elsie Barbara Hill for proofreading.

To all of them my sincere thanks,
Aleksander J. Potočnik

www.ingramcontent.com/pod-product-compliance
Lightning Source LLC
Chambersburg PA
CBHW071704040426
42446CB00011B/1907